CLAIM - EVIDENCE - ANALYSIS

Paragraphs written by Gwendolyn A., 9th Grade Student. These are three unedited versions of the same paragraph. The paragraphs show how students can expand their writing as their abilities grow once they have learned *The Baran Method*.

Lou Gehrig's message to his fans was to be thankful. Lou Gehrig states, "I have been in ballparks for 17 years and never received anything but kindness and encouragement from you fans." Through this quote, Gehrig is saying that he appreciates the encouragement his fans have been giving him over the years.

Lou Gehrig's message to his fans was to be thankful. In his farewell speech, he stated many blessings he had been given. Lou Gehrig states, "I have been in ballparks for 17 years and never received anything but kindness and encouragement from you fans." Through this quote, Gehrig is saying that he appreciates the encouragement his fans have been giving him over the years. Consequently, he wants to encourage his fans and peers to remember the good things we have been given.

Lou Gehrig's message to his fans was to be thankful. In his farewell speech, he stated many blessings he had been given. Lou Gehrig states, "I have been in ballparks for 17 years and never received anything but kindness and encouragement from you fans." Through this quote, Gehrig is saying that he appreciates the encouragement his fans have been giving him over the years. Additionally, he tells us, "Look at these grand men. Who wouldn't consider it the highlight of his career to associate with them for even one day? Sure, I'm lucky." In this passage, Lou is stating that he has worked with many famous men in the world of baseball, but he does not take it for granted. Consequently, he wants to encourage his fans and peers to remember the good things we have been given.

THE BARAN METHOD WORKBOOK

Tenth Grade

GREG BARAN

Table of Contents

Preface

In our personal and business lives, the need to communicate effectively has become paramount. Today, most of our written communications are electronic, especially in the professional world. This speed of communication magnifies the need to communicate clearly. The foundation for opportunity and success in the professional world begins at the elementary level and continues throughout the educational process. Well-written paragraphs and essays created early in our lives form the foundation for the reports we write later that directly affect our upward mobility in the professional world. Consequently, being able to write clearly and effectively is the key to our children's success.

This workbook is an adjunct to *The Baran Method: Writing for Success*. *The Baran Method* lays the groundwork for effective communication and writing because it offers a *clear* understanding of the structures of *clear* communication. This workbook builds on the concepts presented in *The Baran Method* by giving the continued practice needed to master the writing process. When a child reads, thinks critically, and then responds to the readings in writing, they set themselves squarely on the path to success.

Everyone can gain this mastery. It's not complicated. Like everything worth doing, it just takes time and practice.

I'm glad you're here. Thanks for allowing me to join you on this journey.

Happy writing,
Greg Baran

P.S. Remember to contact us if you have any questions. No question is insignificant—we love all of them! You can email us at greg@thebaranmethod.com or call Ph. (760) 459-5597. Plus, we also offer online writing courses at thebaranmethod.com. We want your kids to succeed!

Instructions

Baran Method definition:

effective writing, v. — to organize ideas and put them on paper or type them in a clear and logical manner.

Practice makes permanent.

The key to teaching writing and learning to write is practice, practice, practice. As a teacher or student, establish the writing goal and the process for achieving the goal. Keep the goal and the process straightforward and easy-to-follow.

Before beginning in the workbook, please do Exercises 1 - 6 in _The Baran Method: Writing for Success_. That's where students will learn the easy-to-use concepts that are the foundation for successful writing: **claim**, **evidence**, and **analysis**, or **CEA**. If students do the exercises first, and then shift over to the workbook, they'll be writing effectively in a short time.

Throughout this process, please keep the **CEA** paragraph map in _The Baran Method: Writing for Success_ close by to help guide students. Start with a three-sentence **CEA** paragraph and keep writing three-sentence paragraphs until your students have gained confidence. Then, add more sentences. An example of the transition from three to five—and then even more sentences—is on the first page of every _Baran Method_ book.

For tenth grade, when a student can write a five-sentence paragraph competently, the paragraph writing goal has been met. Essay goals can be found later in this section. An added objective for students would be to extend their paragraphs by adding more **supporting detail**, **evidence**, and/or **analysis**. A solid first-step toward extending a paragraph is to include more **analysis**.

Keep in mind, if a student is struggling to write a three-sentence **CEA** paragraph, focus solely on writing a **claim**. Then work on adding **evidence** and **analysis** when your student is ready. Meeting students at their current level and ability is important for their writing success.

To help guide students, paragraph examples for the first four assignments are located at the back of this workbook. The modeling of effective writing is another key to every student's writing success. Students don't learn to write by reading about how to write, they learn through observation, demonstration, and practice. Seeing writing examples helps students understand what a desired writing product might look like for them. This eliminates confusion and helps students throughout the writing process.

Some may be concerned that students will simply copy the model. However, most student writers innately understand that the model is just that, a model to guide their writing. Yet even if a student does copy a model word-for-word, this will not lead to a negative outcome. After a short time, the student will understand the structure of the model and the goal for their writing. Students will then understand how to incorporate the model into their own writing.

To make teaching even easier, use *The Baran Method Teacher Edition*. *The Baran Method Teacher Edition* includes every assignment in this workbook, writing examples for every assignment, and for your convenience, the **evidence** has already been highlighted in **green**. Plus, our Teacher Edition has example essays to make teaching essay writing easier. There's more information on essay writing later in this section.

While students are writing, please have them write or type in color with blue, green, and red pens or font. The colors are absolutely essential—they help students organize their ideas and remember how to work with CEA.

In regard to writing drafts, many teachers have students write their rough drafts in a composition notebook and then write their final draft in this workbook. That's an excellent way to allow for revision work before the final draft is completed.

This is the suggested process for working on an assignment:

1. Read the writing prompt that accompanies the assignment to become familiar with what students will be doing.
2. For the first four readings, read each writing example at the back of this workbook before working with students. Use the writing examples to help guide student writing. Alternatively, use *The Baran Method Teacher Edition,* which includes every assignment in this workbook, writing examples, and for teacher convenience, the **evidence** has already been highlighted.
3. Read the assignment.
4. Write the **claim** (finding the **evidence** before writing the **claim** is fine).
5. Highlight the **evidence**.
6. Finish writing a *Baran Method* **CEA** paragraph.

At any age, the primary objective when we read is to find the main idea, so the writing prompts largely focus on this skill. However, changing the prompt may be desired for a particular assignment, so this should be done when needed.

Regarding a writing schedule, regular practice time is very helpful. Also, there are twenty assignments in each workbook. A suggested schedule is to do one assignment every other week. By just doing the assignments in the workbook, students will complete twenty readings and accompanying paragraphs. That's enough to build mastery while not overwhelming and "burning out" students. Add in any writing for the English Language Arts curriculum students are working on and that number might double, which is why we don't want to overload students. Over the course of the year, this amount of reading and writing will build a solid foundation for all future writing.

In addition, after students can competently write a paragraph, the natural progression is to write an essay. This transition can be very difficult for some students. However, *The Baran Method* takes a majority of the pain out of essay writing by showing students how to organize their terrific ideas. Like the CEA Paragraph Map, the CEA Essay Maps *show the purpose and placement for each sentence in an essay so writers can focus on what to say and not worry about where to say it.*

When students are introduced to the essay maps in *The Baran Method: Writing for Success*, they will see that a CEA paragraph will become the body paragraph in an essay. This key feature is an integral part of *The Baran Method*. By practicing writing CEA paragraphs, students are directly preparing themselves to write the body paragraphs in an essay. This makes essay writing much easier since students are simply building on skills they've already mastered. Remember, while using an essay map, the objective is for students to follow the map sentence-by-sentence as they write their essay.

In addition, using *The Baran Method* essay examples to guide instruction is extremely useful and helpful. Essay examples that correspond to three of the essay prompts at the back of this workbook are in the Teacher Edition. Also, one of the corresponding essays is in the "Workbook Writing Examples" folder in the Online Resources at thebaranmethod.com/resources-access. More essay examples can be found in *The Baran Method: Writing for Success* textbook.

A suggested writing goal would be for tenth grade students to write five to six essays over the course of the year. If possible, more is preferred. This will give students enough practice so that they are headed toward becoming a *Writing Ninja* as they enter eleventh grade.

Essay prompts are provided in the APPENDIX of this workbook. There is also a list of helpful websites, and most importantly, the paragraph writing examples are located in the APPENDIX.

Activities While Reading

These activities will help students further understand and practice working with the concepts of claim, evidence, and analysis while also helping to build their reading comprehension and annotation skills.

- For the non-fiction articles, have a blue, green, and red highlighter at the ready and highlight the author's claim, evidence, and analysis. Students may also want to highlight the thesis in yellow, just like *The Baran Method* essay maps.

- For fiction, the **claim**, **evidence**, and **analysis** is not as apparent. However, having a highlighter ready to highlight evidence of the author's message or theme is a great idea.

- Have a pen or pencil ready to annotate and write notes in the margins of each text.

- Use a pen or writing implement of choice and underline or circle transition words.

- Have students read the assignments out loud. This will help them build fluency, which will help with overall reading comprehension.

- Have students read their own writing out loud. This will help them check their writing for clarity and grammar errors.

- *When possible, have students do all of these activities with each other's written paragraphs and essays.*

ASSIGNMENTS

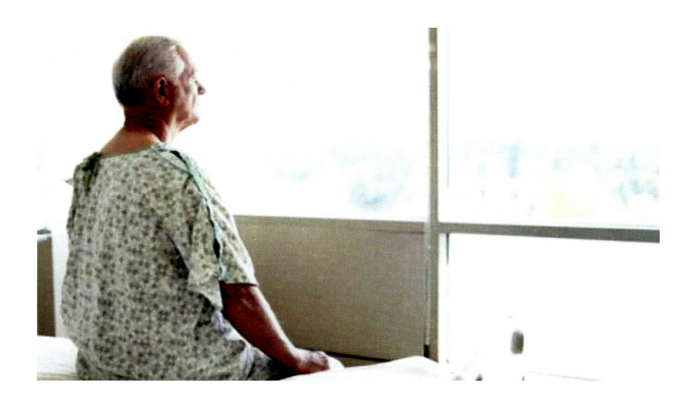

Hospital Window

Two men, both seriously ill, occupied the same hospital room.

One man was allowed to sit up in his bed for an hour each afternoon to help drain the fluid from his lungs. His bed was next to the room's only window. The other man had to spend all of his time flat on his back.

The two men talked for hours on end. They spoke of their wives and families, their homes, their jobs, their involvement in the military service, and where they had been on vacation.

And every afternoon when the man in the bed by the window could sit up, he would pass the time by describing to his roommate all the things he could see outside the window. The man in the other bed began to live for those one-hour periods when his world would be broadened and enlivened by all the activity and the color of the world outside the hospital window.

The window overlooked a park with a lovely lake. Ducks and swans played on the water while children sailed their model boats. Young lovers walked arm in arm through flowers of every color of the rainbow. Grand old trees graced the landscape, and a fine view of the city skyline could be seen in the distance.

As the man by the window described all of this in excellent detail, the man on the other side of the room would close his eyes and imagine the beautiful scene.

One warm afternoon, the man by the window described a parade passing by below. Although the other man couldn't hear the band, he could see it in his mind as the gentleman by the window described it.

Weeks went by. One morning, a nurse arrived to bring water for their baths and found the lifeless body of the man by the window. He had died peacefully in his sleep. She was saddened and called the hospital attendants to take the body away.

As soon as it seemed appropriate in a few days, the other man asked if he could be moved next to the window. The nurse was happy to make the switch, and after making sure he was comfortable, she left the man alone. Slowly, painfully, he propped himself up on one elbow to take his first look at the world outside.

Finally, he would have the joy of seeing it for himself.

He moved slowly to turn and look out the window beside the bed. The window faced a blank brick wall.

Later that day, the nurse came back, and the man asked the nurse what would have caused his deceased roommate to describe such wonderful things outside the window.

The nurse answered that the man was blind and could not even see the wall. She softly replied, "Maybe he just wanted to encourage you."

Discussion Questions:
1. Why didn't the blind man tell his friend he was blind?
2. What caused the two men to become close friends?
3. What did the blind man "see" in the park?

Writing Prompt:

When an author writes a story, their goal is to entertain while also sharing an idea. When we read, we want to be like a detective and find this idea. For fictional stories, this idea is frequently called the theme. Author's also include messages, morals, and lessons. What is the theme of "Hospital Window" and what can we learn from this theme?

_____

_____

_____

Crater of Fire

Hidden in the vast and arid Karakum Desert in Turkmenistan lies what is known as the Crater of Fire, or for those who prefer a bit more drama, *The Door to Hell*. Reminiscent of a Hollywood disaster or horror film, the crater is filled with spouting flames and glowing orange rocks, which makes it easy to understand why this pit was given such a dramatic nickname.

Similar to films where the earth is put in danger by a mad scientist or human error, the crater owes its origins to humans, although to their credit, the people who accidentally created the crater were simply well-intentioned scientists and engineers. Nevertheless, the moral still stands—it's not a good idea to mess with nature.

So, how did *The Door to Hell* get there? The Karakum Desert covers much of the country of Turkmenistan, which is located south of Russia and east of China. In the west, the country is bordered by the Caspian Sea. Before the Soviet Union dissolved in 1991, Turkmenistan was a state in the Soviet Union. However, the small state became its own sovereign nation with Russia's dissolution.

When the country became independent of the Soviet Union, the country was thrown into disarray since they had to govern themselves now, which forced a reorganization of governmental power and societal norms, which were formerly controlled by Russia.

However, one thing that remained the same and allowed for a fairly quick stabilization within the country was their production of natural gas. This small country is the sixth largest producer of natural gas in the world, and countries like China and Russia buy vast quantities of gas from this small nation every year.

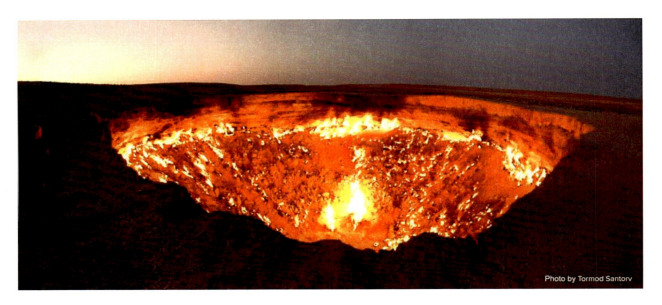
Photo by Tormod Santorv

Fifty years ago, while Turkmenistan was still part of the Soviet Union, Soviet geologists and engineers in search of crude oil trekked to a region of the Karakum Desert called Darvaza.

The researchers had traveled to Darvaza because geologists had theorized that there was a rich oil reserve under the desert. Once the specific location for drilling was chosen, an oil rig was erected in the desert and drilling soon began. However, to the engineers' surprise and dismay, they quickly realized that they weren't drilling into an oil reserve. Instead, they were drilling into a natural gas pocket. Their massive and immensely heavy oil rig began sinking into the earth, and within days, the rig collapsed into the massive gas pocket.

The Door to Hell had been opened.

Unfortunately for the beleaguered Russian scientists, they soon realized that they had an even bigger problem on their hands. The collapse of the Darvaza crater had created similar effects across the area, and smaller craters had formed and were now also leaking gas into the desert.

In addition, the gas wasn't just escaping at minor rates, fissures in the earth were rapidly releasing pressurized natural gas into the air and into the soil at an extremely high volume.

The situation quickly became a serious problem since scientists knew the effects the natural gas would have on the environment and the people living in both nearby and far-off regions. Natural gas consists largely of methane, which absorbs oxygen. This meant that as the gas cloud spread, it would become harder and harder for people, animals, and plants to survive in the region. Researchers were very much afraid that they would have to evacuate all nearby towns and cities and prepare for an even larger evacuation as the gas continued to pour through the region.

Photo by Benjamin Goetzinger

The scientists' fears started to manifest like a bad Hollywood horror movie when animals in the area began to die several days after the collapse of the rig.

But that's also when researchers landed on what seemed like a logical course of action: gas burns, so light the crater on fire. The scientists believed the gas would burn off in a matter of days or weeks. That was fifty years ago.

Since then, *The Door to Hell* has never stopped burning. In fact, the large bowl-shaped crater that exists today is located exactly where the oil rig collapsed into the ground. Now, the crater left behind measures 230 feet in diameter by 65 feet deep.

To complicate matters, scientists are not sure why the pockets have never burned out. Most theories suggest that the Darvaza crater is connected to a much larger field of natural gas below and beside the crater.

But scientists can't access this field because they're afraid they might create a larger catastrophe than *The Door to Hell*. They've theorized that if they accidentally connect this crater to a larger gas field, they could create an explosion that would encompass the entire region.

So, for a solution, Turkmenistan did the next best thing: they gave the crater a Hollywood ending by making it a tourist attraction.

For years, the crater was just left out in the open. You could walk up to the lip of the crater, peer over the edge, or as a few scientists and adventurers have done, even go down into it, albeit with appropriate gas masks and protective fire suits since the crater is loaded with off-gassing fires and scalding hot rocks.

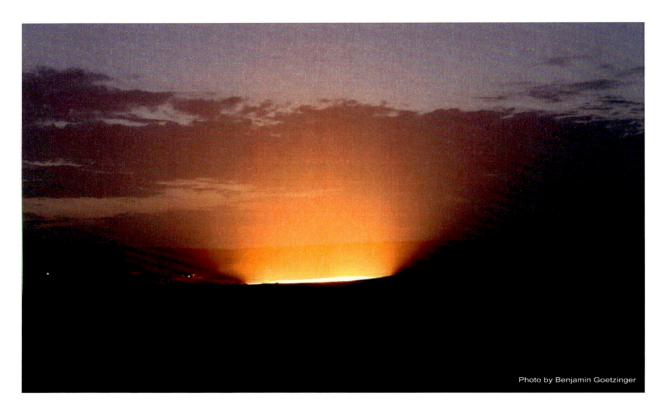

However, the facilities surrounding the crater have been updated over the past few years since so many people love to visit the crater. Thousands of tourists now visit Darvaza every year to take a peek at the otherworldly phenomenon. Because of the increased tourism, there's now a paved road leading to the crater, a parking lot, picnic areas, and even a safety rail.

Over the years, some Turkmenistan officials have occasionally suggested that it would be safer to close the crater. Yet like a horror film that draws our attention even though we know it's going to scare us, people flock to *The Door to Hell* like a moth to light. That heavy flow of tourism will help to keep the door open.

Hopefully, though, visitors will learn from the lesson the crater provides: nature has its own will, and it's a good idea to be cautious when interacting with it.

Discussion Questions:
1. Where is the Crater of Fire located?
2. What circumstances created this phenomenon?
3. Which is a better solution: putting the fire out, leaving it as a tourist attraction, or finding some other use for the crater?

Writing Prompt:

Articles always have a main idea. When we read, we want to be like a detective and find the author's main idea. What is the main idea of this article?

I'm Nobody! Who are you?

By Emily Dickinson

I'm Nobody! Who are you?
Are you – Nobody – too?
Then there's a pair of us!
Don't tell! They'd advertise – you know!

How dreary – to be – Somebody!
How public – like a Frog –
To tell one's name – the livelong June –
To an admiring Bog!

Discussion Questions:
1. How do you feel after reading this poem?
2. What is the "admiring Bog" and why does Dickinson compare this "Bog" to frogs? Do you relate to Dickinson's perspective?
3. Who was Emily Dickinson?

Writing Prompt:

Poetry can be described as "word art." Poets want to inspire, entertain, and share a message. Poets use specific words, ideas, and word placement to accomplish this goal. Emily Dickinson is famous for her insight into human psychology while using humor and satire to convey her ideas. Dickinson creates a metaphor by comparing society to a group of frogs. Why does she make this comparison and how does it help her convey her message?

_____

_____

_____

_____

_____

Argument/Persuasive Writing: Junk Food Ban

Preparing a healthy meal for lunch can be a lot of work. As a result, many students simply eat easily prepared junk food like pizza for lunch and wash it down with a soda.

Junk food is generally considered food that is low in nutritional value and high in fat, calories, sugar, and salt content. While eating junk food occasionally may not be harmful to a teen's health, research has shown that doing so on a daily basis can have a detrimental impact on a student's well-being. For this reason, some schools have banned junk food from campus.

Proponents of banning junk food cite research that shows fresh vegetables, fruits, and meats are much healthier than pre-cooked foods, which have a long list of added ingredients and preservatives. Moreover, they argue that a diet which is free of junk food has several benefits for students, including maintaining a healthy weight, building stronger bones, fewer intestinal issues, and increased memory, recall, and concentration.

However, opponents assert that junk food isn't the culprit. Instead, they think that choosing to eat too much of it is the problem. Moreover, opponents argue that among the benefits of junk food are its convenience and the speed and ease with which it can be prepared, which they assert is advantageous in a school setting.

They also cite research that demonstrates it takes deliberate and concentrated commitment, work, and effort for a school to switch over to a healthy food model. They say that students want to eat healthier, but schools have to deliver on that promise.

What do you think?

Writing Prompt:
　　Is it a good idea to ban junk food from schools? For evidence, state your experience, conduct research, conduct an interview, or include a survey.

_____

_____

_____

_____

_____

_____

_____

_____

_____

The Monkey's Paw

By W. W. Jacobs

PART ONE

Outside, the night was cold and wet, but in the small living room the curtains were closed and the fire burned brightly. Father and son were playing chess; the father, whose ideas about the game involved some very unusual moves, putting his king into such sharp and unnecessary danger that it even brought comment from the white-haired old lady knitting quietly by the fire.

"Listen to the wind," said Mr. White who, having seen a mistake that could cost him the game after it was too late, was trying to stop his son from seeing it.

"I'm listening," said the son, seriously studying the board as he stretched out his hand. "Check."

"I should hardly think that he'll come tonight," said his father, with his hand held in the air over the board.

"Mate," replied the son. "That's the worst of living so far out," cried Mr. White with sudden and unexpected violence; "Of all the awful out of the way places to live in, this is the worst. Can't walk on the footpath without getting stuck in the mud, and the road's a river. I don't know what the people are thinking about. I suppose they think it doesn't matter because only two houses in the road have people in them."

"Never mind, dear," said his wife calmly, "perhaps you'll win the next one."

Mr. White looked up sharply, just in time to see a knowing look between mother and son. The words died away on his lips, and he hid a guilty smile in his thin grey beard. "There he is," said Herbert White as the gate banged shut loudly and heavy footsteps came toward the door.

The old man rose quickly, and opening the door, was heard telling the new arrival how sorry he was for his recent loss.

The new arrival talked about his sadness, so that Mrs. White said, "Tut, tut!" and coughed gently as her husband entered the room followed by a tall, heavy built, strong-looking man, whose skin had the healthy reddish colour associated with outdoor life and whose eyes showed that he could be a dangerous enemy.

"Sergeant-Major Morris," he said, introducing him to his wife and his son, Herbert.

The Sergeant-Major shook hands and, taking the offered seat by the fire, watched with satisfaction as Mr. White got out whiskey and glasses. After the third glass, his eyes got brighter and he began to talk.

The little family circle listened with growing interest to this visitor from distant parts, as he squared his broad shoulders in the chair and spoke of wild scenes and brave acts; of wars and strange peoples.

"Twenty-one years of it," said Mr. White, looking at his wife and son. "When he went away, he was a thin young man. Now look at him."

"He doesn't look to have taken much harm." said Mrs. White politely.

"I'd like to go to India myself," said the old man, just to look around a bit, "you know."

"Better where you are," said the Sergeant-Major, shaking his head. He put down the empty glass and, sighing softly, shook it again.

"I should like to see those old temples and fakirs and the street entertainers," said the old man. "What was that you started telling me the other day about a monkey's paw or something, Morris?"

"Nothing." said the soldier quickly. "At least, nothing worth hearing."

"Monkey's paw?" said Mrs. White curiously.

"Well, it's just a bit of what you might call magic, perhaps," said the Sergeant-Major, without first stopping to think. His three listeners leaned forward excitedly. Deep in thought, the visitor put his empty glass to his lips and then set it down again.

Mr. White filled it for him again. "To look at it," said the Sergeant-Major, feeling about in his pocket, "it's just an ordinary little paw, dried to a mummy."

He took something out of his pocket and held it out for them. Mrs. White drew back with a look of disgust, but her son, taking it, examined it curiously.

"And what is there special about it?" asked Mr. White as he took it from his son, and having examined it, placed it upon the table.

"It had a spell put on it by an old fakir," said the Sergeant-Major, "a very holy man. He wanted to show that fate ruled people's lives, and that those who tried to change it would be sorry. He put a spell on it so that three different men could each have three wishes from it."

The way he told the story showed that he truly believed it and his listeners became aware that their light laughter was out of place and had hurt him a little.

"Well, why don't you have three, sir?" said Herbert, cleverly.

The soldier looked at him the way that the middle-aged usually look at disrespectful youth. "I have," he said quietly, and his face whitened.

"And did you really have the three wishes granted?" asked Mrs. White.

"I did," said the Sergeant-Major, and his glass tapped against his strong teeth.

"And has anybody else wished?" continued the old lady.

"Yes," was the reply, "the first man had his three wishes. I don't know what the first two were, but the third was for death. That's how I got the paw."

His voice was so serious that the group fell quiet.

"If you've had your three wishes, it's no good to you now then, Morris," said the old man at last. "What do you keep it for?"

The soldier shook his head. "Fancy, I suppose," he said slowly. "I did have some idea of selling it, but I don't think I will. It has caused me enough trouble already. Besides, people won't buy. They think it's just a story, some of them; and those who do think anything of it want to try it first and pay me afterward."

"If you could have another three wishes," said the old man, watching him carefully, "would you have them?"

"I don't know," said the other. "I don't know."

He took the paw, and holding it between his front finger and thumb, suddenly threw it upon the fire.

Mr. White, with a slight cry, quickly bent down and took it off.

"Better let it burn," said the soldier sadly, but in a way that let them know he believed it to be true.

"If you don't want it, Morris," said the other, "give it to me."

"I won't," said his friend with stubborn determination. "I threw it on the fire. If you keep it, don't hold me responsible for what happens. Throw it on the fire like a sensible man."

The other shook his head and examined his possession closely. "How do you do it?" he asked.

"Hold it up in your right hand, and state your wish out loud so that you can be heard," said the Sergeant-Major, "but I warn you of what might happen."

"Sounds like the 'Arabian Nights'", said Mrs. White, as she rose and began to set the dinner. "Don't you think you might wish for four pairs of hands for me?"

Her husband drew the talisman from his pocket, and all three laughed loudly as the Sergeant-Major, with a look of alarm on his face, caught him by the arm. "If you must wish," he demanded, "wish for something sensible."

Mr. White dropped it back in his pocket, and placing chairs, motioned his friend to the table. In the business of dinner, the talisman was partly forgotten, and afterward the three sat fascinated as they listened to more of the soldier's adventures in India.

"If the tale about the monkey's paw is not more truthful than those he has been telling us," said Herbert, as the door closed behind their guest, just in time to catch the last train, "we shan't make much out of it."

"Did you give anything for it, father?" asked Mrs. White, watching her husband closely.

"A little," said he, colouring slightly, "he didn't want it, but I made him take it. And he pressed me again to throw it away."

"Not likely!" said Herbert, with pretended horror. "Why, we're going to be rich, and famous, and happy." Smiling, he said, "Wish to be a king, father, to begin with; then mother can't complain all the time." He ran quickly around the table, chased by the laughing Mrs. White armed with a piece of cloth.

Mr. White took the paw from his pocket and eyed it doubtfully. "I don't know what to wish for, and that's a fact," he said slowly. "It seems to me I've got all I want."

"If you only paid off the house, you'd be quite happy, wouldn't you?" said Herbert, with his hand on his shoulder. "Well, wish for two hundred pounds, then that'll just do it."

His father, smiling, and with an embarrassed look for his foolishness in believing the soldier's story, held up the talisman. Herbert, with a serious face, spoiled only by a quick smile to his mother, sat down at the piano and struck a few grand chords.

"I wish for two hundred pounds," said the old man clearly.

A fine crash from the piano greeted his words, broken by a frightened cry from the old man. His wife and son ran toward him.

"It moved," he cried, with a look of horror at the object as it lay on the floor. "As I wished, it twisted in my hand like a snake."

"Well, I don't see the money," said his son, as he picked it up and placed it on the table, "and I bet I never shall."

"It must have been your imagination, father," said his wife, regarding him worriedly.

He shook his head. "Never mind, though; there's no harm done, but it gave me a shock all the same."

They sat down by the fire again while the two men finished their pipes. Outside, the wind was higher than ever, and the old man jumped nervously at the sound of a door banging upstairs. An unusual and depressing silence settled on all three, which lasted until the old couple got up to go to bed.

"I expect you'll find the cash tied up in a big bag in the middle of your bed," said Herbert, as he wished them goodnight, "and something horrible sitting on top of your wardrobe watching you as you pocket your ill-gotten money."

Herbert, who normally had a playful nature and didn't like to take things too seriously, sat alone in the darkness looking into the dying fire. He saw faces in it; the last so horrible and so monkey-like that he stared at it in amazement. It became so clear that, with a nervous laugh, he felt on the table for a glass containing some water to throw over it. His hand found the monkey's paw, and with a little shake of his body, he wiped his hand on his coat and went up to bed.

PART TWO

In the brightness of the wintry sun next morning as it streamed over the breakfast table, he laughed at his fears. The room felt as it always had and there was an air of health and happiness which was not there the previous night. The dirty, dried-up little paw was thrown on the cabinet with a carelessness which indicated no great belief in what good it could do.

"I suppose all old soldiers are the same," said Mrs. White. "The idea of our listening to such nonsense! How could wishes be granted in these days? And if they could, how could two hundred pounds hurt you, father?"

"Might drop on his head from the sky," said Herbert.

"Morris said the things happened so naturally," said his father, "that you might if you so wished not see the relationship."

"Well, don't break into the money before I come back," said Herbert as he rose from the table to go to work. "I'm afraid it'll turn you into a mean, greedy old man, and we shall have to tell everyone that we don't know you."

His mother laughed, and following him to the door, watched him go down the road, and returning to the breakfast table, she felt very happy at the expense of her husband's readiness to believe such stories. All of which did not prevent her from hurrying to the door at the postman's knock nor, when she found that the post brought only a bill, talking about how Sergeant-Majors can develop bad drinking habits after they leave the army.

"Herbert will have some more of his funny remarks, I expect, when he comes home," she said as they sat at dinner.

"I know," said Mr. White, pouring himself out some beer, "but for all that, the thing moved in my hand; that I'll swear to."

"You thought it did," said the old lady, trying to calm him.

"I say it did," replied the other. "There was no thought about it; I had just—what's the matter?"

His wife made no reply. She was watching the mysterious movements of a man outside, who, looking in an undecided fashion at the house, appeared to be trying to make up his mind to enter. In mental connection with the two hundred pounds, she noticed that the stranger was well dressed and wore a silk hat of shiny newness. Three times he stopped briefly at the gate and then walked on again. The fourth time he stood with his hand upon it, and then with sudden firmness of mind pushed it open and walked up the path.

Mrs. White, at the same moment, placed her hands behind her, hurriedly untied the strings of her apron, and put it under the cushion of her chair. She brought the stranger, who seemed a little uncomfortable, into the room. He looked at her in a way that said there was something about his purpose that he wanted to keep secret, and seemed to be thinking of something else as the old lady said she was sorry for the appearance of the room and her husband's coat, which he usually wore in the garden. She then waited as patiently as her sex would permit for him to state his business, but he was at first strangely silent.

"I—was asked to call," he said at last, and bent down and picked a piece of cotton from his trousers. "I come from 'Maw and Meggins.' "

The old lady jumped suddenly, as in alarm. "Is anything the matter?" she asked breathlessly.

"Has anything happened to Herbert? What is it? What is it?"

Her husband spoke before he could answer. "There, there mother," he said hurriedly.

"Sit down and don't jump to a conclusion. You've not brought bad news, I'm sure sir," and eyed the other, expecting that it was bad news, but hoping he was wrong.

"I'm sorry—" began the visitor.

"Is he hurt?" demanded the mother wildly.

The visitor lowered and raised his head once in agreement. "Badly hurt," he said quietly, "but he is not in any pain."

"Oh, thank God!" said the old woman, pressing her hands together tightly. "Thank God for that! Thank—" She broke off as the tragic meaning of the part about him not being in pain came to her.

The man had turned his head slightly so as not to look directly at her, but she saw the awful truth in his face. She caught her breath, and turning to her husband, who did not yet understand the man's meaning, laid her shaking hand on his. There was a long silence.

"He was caught in the machinery," said the visitor at length in a low voice.

"Caught in the machinery," repeated Mr. White, too shocked to think clearly.

He sat staring out the window, and taking his wife's hand between his own, pressed it as he used to do when he was trying to win her love in the time before they were married, nearly forty years before.

"He was the only one left to us," he said, turning gently to the visitor. "It is hard."

The other coughed, and rising, walked slowly to the window. "The firm wishes me to pass on their great sadness about your loss," he said, without looking round. "I ask that you please understand that I am only their servant and simply doing what they told me to do."

There was no reply; the old woman's face was white, her eyes staring, and her breath unheard; on the husband's face was a look such as his friend the Sergeant-Major might have carried into his first battle.

"I was to say that Maw and Meggins accept no responsibility," continued the other. "But, although they don't believe that they have a legal requirement to make a payment to you for your loss, in view of your son's services, they wish to present you with a certain sum."

Mr. White dropped his wife's hand, and rising to his feet, stared with a look of horror at his visitor. His dry lips shaped the words, "How much?"

"Two hundred pounds," was the answer.

Without hearing his wife's scream, the old man smiled weakly, put out his hands like a blind man, and fell, a senseless mass, to the floor.

PART THREE

In the huge new cemetery, some two miles away, the old people buried their dead, and came back to the house, which was now full of shadows and silence. It was all over so quickly that at first they could hardly realize it, and remained in a state of waiting for something else to happen—something else which was to lighten this load, too heavy for old hearts to bear.

But the days passed, and they realized that they had to accept the situation—the hopeless acceptance of the old. Sometimes they hardly said a word to each other, for now they had nothing to talk about, and their days were long to tiredness.

It was about a week after that the old man, waking suddenly in the night, stretched out his hand and found himself alone. The room was in darkness, and he could hear the sound of his wife crying quietly at the window.

He raised himself in bed and listened. "Come back," he said tenderly. "You will be cold."

"It is colder for my son," said the old woman, who began crying again.

The sounds of crying died away on his ears. The bed was warm, and his eyes heavy with sleep. He slept lightly at first, and then was fully asleep until a sudden wild cry from his wife woke him with a start.

"THE PAW!" she cried wildly. "THE MONKEY'S PAW!"

He started up in alarm. "What's the matter?"

She almost fell as she hurried across the room toward him. "I want it," she said quietly. "You've not destroyed it?"

"It's in the living room, on the shelf above the fireplace," he replied. "Why?"

She cried and laughed together, and bending over, kissed his cheek. "I only just thought of it," she said. "Why didn't I think of it before? Why didn't you think of it?"

"Think of what?" he questioned.

"The other two wishes," she replied quickly. "We've only had one."

"Was not that enough?" he demanded angrily.

"No," she cried excitedly; "We'll have one more. Go down and get it quickly, and wish our boy alive again."

The man sat up in bed and threw the blankets from his shaking legs. "Good God, you are mad!" he cried, struck with horror.

"Get it," she said, breathing quickly, "get it quickly, and wish—Oh my boy, my boy!"

Her husband struck a match and lit the candle. "Get back to bed he said," his voice shaking. "You don't know what you are saying."

"We had the first wish granted," said the old woman, desperately, "why not the second?"

"A c-c-coincidence," said the old man.

"Go get it and wish," cried his wife, shaking with excitement.

The old man turned and looked at her, and his voice shook. "He has been dead ten days, and besides he—I would not tell you before, but—I could only recognize him by his clothing. If he was too terrible for you to see then, how now?"

"Bring him back," cried the old woman, and pulled him towards the door. "Do you think I fear the child I have nursed?"

He went down in the darkness, and felt his way to the living room, and then to the fireplace. The talisman was in its place on the shelf, and then a horrible fear came over him that the unspoken wish might bring the broken body of his son before him before he could escape from the room. He caught his breath as he found that he had lost the direction of the door. His forehead cold with sweat, he felt his way round the table and along the walls until he found himself at the bottom of the stairs with the evil thing in his hand.

Even his wife's face seemed changed as he entered the room. It was white and expectant, and to his fears seemed to have an unnatural look upon it. He was afraid of her.

"WISH!" she cried in a strong voice.

"It is foolish and wicked," he said weakly.

"WISH!" repeated his wife.

He raised his hand. "I wish my son alive again."

The talisman fell to the floor, and he looked at it fearfully. Then he sank into a chair and the old woman, with burning eyes, walked to the window and opened the curtains. He sat until he could no longer bear the cold, looking up from time to time at the figure of his wife staring through the window. The candle, which had almost burned to the bottom, was throwing moving shadows around the room. When the candle finally went out, the old man, with an unspeakable sense of relief at the failure of the talisman, went slowly back to his bed, and a minute afterward the old woman came silently and lay without movement beside him. Neither spoke, but lay silently listening to the ticking of the clock. They heard nothing else other than the normal night sounds.

The darkness was depressing, and after lying for some time building up his courage, the husband took the box of matches, and lighting one, went downstairs for another candle. At the foot of the stairs, the match went out, and he stopped to light another; and at the same moment, a knock sounded on the front door.

It was so quiet that it could only be heard downstairs, as if the one knocking wanted to keep their coming a secret. The matches fell from his hand. He stood motionless, not even breathing, until the knock was repeated. Then he turned and ran quickly back to his room and closed the door behind him.

A third knock sounded through the house.

"WHAT'S THAT?" cried the old woman, sitting up quickly.

"A rat," said the old man shakily—"A rat. It passed me on the stairs."

His wife sat up in bed, listening.

A loud knock echoed through the house.

"It's Herbert!" she screamed. "It's Herbert!"

She ran to the door, but her husband was there before her, and catching her by the arm, held her tightly.

"What are you going to do?" he asked in a low, scared voice.

"It's my boy; it's Herbert!" she cried, struggling automatically. "I forgot it was two miles away. What are you holding me for? Let go. I must open the door."

"For God's sake, don't let it in," cried the old man, shaking with fear.

"You're afraid of your own son," she cried, struggling. "Let me go. I'm coming, Herbert, I'm coming."

There was another knock, and another. The old woman, with a sudden pull, broke free and ran from the room. Her husband followed to the top of the stairs and called after her as she hurried down. He heard the chain pulled back and the bottom lock open.

Then the old woman's voice, desperate and breathing heavily. "The top lock," she cried loudly. "Come down. I can't reach it."

But her husband was on his hands and knees, feeling around wildly on the floor in search of the paw. If only he could find it before the thing outside got in.

The knocks came very quickly now, echoing through the house, and he heard the noise of his wife moving a chair and putting it down against the door. He heard the movement of the lock as she began to open it, and at the same moment he found the monkey's paw and frantically breathed his third and last wish.

The knocking stopped suddenly, although the echoes of it were still in the house. He heard the chair being pulled back, and the door opened. A cold wind blew up the staircase, and a long loud cry of disappointment and pain from his wife gave him the courage to run down to her side, and then to the gate. The streetlight opposite shone on a quiet and deserted road.

Discussion Questions:

1. Why did the old fakir create the monkey's paw?

2. When the representative from Maw and Meggins shows up, how do we know he will be delivering bad news?

3. What do you think would have happened if Mrs. White had opened the door?

Writing Prompt:

When an author writes a story, their goal is to entertain while also sharing an

idea. When we read, we want to be like a detective and find this idea. For fictional stories, this idea is frequently called the theme. Author's also include messages, morals, and lessons. W. W. Jacobs' classic, spooky tale has been a standard for over one hundred years. What moral or lesson does Jacobs share in this story?

_____

_____

_____

_____

_____

_____

_____

_____

_____

_____

_____

_____

_____

Photo by Matthew Yohe

Steve Jobs: A Brilliant Mind

Steve Jobs brought smartphones to the world and changed the way we interact and communicate with each other. His legacy, built on the phones, computers, and entertainment he created, will last for generations.

Jobs started on his entrepreneurial path while just a young boy. Jobs was born in San Francisco on February 24, 1955, and he grew up in Mountain View, California, with the parents who adopted him, Paul and Clara Jobs.

Jobs spent his entire childhood in this part of California that would come to be known as Silicon Valley decades later. One of his favorite hobbies was working on electronics with his father in their garage workshop. Jobs had an obsessive fascination with electronics, and he loved pulling radios and televisions apart and putting them back together. His father was continually amazed at Steve's ability to understand how parts fit together and his ability to make suggestions about how design improvements could be made to any device.

While in high school, Jobs' fascination with electronics led him to become friends with another technology savant named Steve Wozniak, who later became Job's business partner. Wozniak had an idea to build his own computer, and Jobs encouraged him to do so.

Over the next few years, Wozniak's personal computer became a success, and the two friends began a computer business. That was the beginning of Apple.

Their first major computer was the Apple I. Jobs soon showed his entrepreneurial initiative and spirit by convincing investors to invest in Apple. With their financial backing, Jobs and Wozniak brought the Apple II to market, and this computer became a huge success. Apple was now a multi-million dollar company that was quickly headed toward becoming a multi-billion dollar company.

Jobs' computers created a seismic shift in society because in order to interact with a computer at the time, the operator had to have knowledge of coding. However, Jobs pushed for Apple's computers to focus on ease-of-use, so their computers were controlled by a mouse and keyboard. This was revolutionary since it allowed everyone to use a computer, whereas before only experts and hobbyists could interact with the devices.

Yet with success came the occasional failure, and Jobs had his share. Apple grew incredibly fast, but Jobs was pushed out by the company when a couple of subsequent computers failed to gain the same dominance as Apple's first computers.

Jobs was not one to give up, and he went on to a subsequent venture, NeXT computers. This company failed a few short years after its inception. The failure was credited to the fact that the computer design and interface were brilliant, but they were just too expensive for everyday users, who were the target market.

Again, Jobs moved on. This time, he purchased a small graphics company in 1985 from *Star Wars* creator, George Lucas. Jobs soon retooled the company's mission and vision and moved them toward film production. Subsequently, Pixar was born. To this day, many people are unaware that the company that creates the lovable and ubiquitous animated films that are watched by families around the world was the brainchild of Steve Jobs.

In 1991, several years after its inception, Pixar received its first Disney contract for a full-length film. Pixar's first animated movie was *Toy Story,* which was a huge success. Jobs parlayed Pixar's success into more movies, capital, and clout. He partnered with Disney for many films, until in 2006, Jobs sold Pixar to Disney for $2.7 billion. By then, Jobs, his genius, and his vision, were in high demand. Apple wanted him back, and he went with the caveat that he would have full control.

But Jobs left an enduring legacy through his work with Pixar. Under Jobs' direction, Pixar changed entertainment forever by altering the way we view animation. His work at Pixar allowed for computer generated imagery to become the norm, rather than the cumbersome and slow-to-produce hand drawings that had been in use by animation companies for over fifty years. This created a universal shift in animation production and proliferation that may never be matched.

After leaving Pixar and returning to Apple, Jobs then changed music forever by coming up with the iPod, which took the world by storm. His digital device could store thousands of songs on a gadget that fit on one's pocket, which was absolutely undreamed of and unheard of before Jobs' vision made this device a reality.

However, the iPod paled in comparison to his next creation, the iPhone. In 2007, Jobs and Apple unveiled the iPhone to the world.

Several years later, in 2013, Apple sold more than 350,000 iPhones a day, still a high-water mark for phone sales. This lone device changed the way we use technology and interact with each other and the world. Indeed, the modern world would look much different if Jobs didn't introduce us to this pocket-sized computer. The iPhone was the first smartphone, and it allowed us to have the internet in our pockets, it turned everyone into photographers, made social media a ubiquitous part of our lives, and made Apple into the wealthiest company in the world.

After the iPhone, Jobs was not only considered a visionary entrepreneur, he was a massive celebrity, and people started calling him the greatest innovator of the past fifty years and the new millennium.

However, in 2011, after years of introducing technology that changed the world, Jobs died of pancreatic cancer. Fortunately, his vision and brilliance still live with us every day. His phones and computers have changed the way we communicate, interact, and live, and not only do we use his devices every day, we are entertained by his ideas daily since Pixar films are regularly enjoyed by families around the world. Jobs' legacy is a lasting legacy. His genius not only changed the world: in many ways, it has changed us.

Discussion Questions:
1. How did Jobs get his start in technology?
2. Name some of Jobs' contributions to society?
3. What is Jobs' legacy?

Writing Prompt:
Articles always have a main idea. When we read, we want to be like a detective and find the author's main idea. What is the main idea of this article?

_____

_____

Photo by Jonas Mohamadi

On Children

By Kahlil Gibran

And a woman who held a babe against her bosom said, Speak to us of Children.
And he said:

Your children are not your children.
They are the sons and daughters of Life's longing for itself.
They come through you but not from you,
And though they are with you yet they belong not to you.

You may give them your love but not your thoughts,
For they have their own thoughts.
You may house their bodies but not their souls,
For their souls dwell in the house of tomorrow, which you cannot visit, not even in your dreams.
You may strive to be like them, but seek not to make them like you.
For life goes not backward nor tarries with yesterday.
You are the bows from which your children as living arrows are sent forth.
The archer sees the mark upon the path of the infinite, and He bends you with His might that His arrows may go swift and far.
Let your bending in the Archer's hand be for gladness;
For even as he loves the arrow that flies, so He loves also the bow that is stable.

Discussion Questions:
1. Did you enjoy reading this poem? Why or why not?
2. What is the purpose of the bow/arrow metaphor?
3. Do you agree with Gibran's perspective?

Writing Prompt:
    Poetry can be described as "word art." Poets want to inspire, entertain, and share a message. Poets use specific words and word placement to accomplish this goal. Gibran creates several metaphors in this poem. Choose one and discuss how the metaphor helps Gibran convey his message?

Argument/Persuasive Writing: Celebrity Role Models

A celebrity's actions, attitudes, and dress have a significant impact on many youths, whether that influence is conscious or unconscious, positive or negative. Throughout history, this is a common theme: we emulate those we look up to.

Today, it requires very little work to see a celebrity's actions and attitudes on display since they're only a "click" away. Yet regardless of era, for an adolescent who is developing their own sense of identity, is it wise to have a celebrity as a role model?

The issue for many arises from a celebrity's positive or negative influence. For instance, proponents of having celebrities as role models cite the constructive influence celebrities can have when they openly discuss the struggles they've faced and worked through, such as mental, emotional, or physical challenges. Advocates argue that when a celebrity talks about the insecurity or trauma they've experienced, this frankness helps teens who have faced similar struggles understand that they're not alone. This can lead to personal acceptance, higher self-esteem, and a higher sense of well-being. Additionally, some celebrities have called attention to certain issues they feel strongly about, which raises public awareness concerning said issue.

However, there is also a negative influence celebrities can have on some teens. For instance, opponents to holding celebrities as role models cite research that shows many teens compare themselves to the celebrity images they see. This research demonstrates that these teens feel highly discontented with themselves if they feel they don't match up. This can lead to issues such as depression or eating disorders. Moreover, some celebrities may unintentionally promote substance use by posting and sharing photos and videos of themselves drinking and smoking. This can lead to teens emulating a celebrity's risk-taking behavior.

For better or worse, the ease-of-access to celebrity behaviors, attitudes, and dress means many teens will be influenced by celebrities, whether positive or negative. Is this helpful or harmful?

Writing Prompt:
Is it a good idea to hold celebrities as role models? For evidence, state your experience, conduct research, conduct an interview, or include a survey.

_____

_____

_____

_____

_____

_____

_____

_____

The Heavenly Christmas Tree

By Fyodor Dostoevsky

I am a novelist, and I suppose I have made up this story. I write "I suppose," though I know for a fact that I have made it up, but yet I keep fancying that it must have happened somewhere at some time, that it must have happened on Christmas Eve in some great town in a time of terrible frost.

I have a vision of a boy, a little boy, six years old or even younger. This boy woke up that morning in a cold, damp cellar. He was dressed in a sort of little dressing-gown and was shivering with cold. There was a cloud of white steam from his breath, and sitting on a box in the corner, he blew the steam out of his mouth and amused himself in his dullness watching it float away. But he was terribly hungry. Several times that morning, he went up to the plank bed where his sick mother was lying on a mattress as thin as a pancake, with some sort of bundle under her head for a pillow. How had she come here? She must have come with her boy from some other town and suddenly fallen ill. The landlady who let the "corners" had been taken two days before to the police station, the lodgers were out and about as the holiday was so near, and the only one left had been lying for the last twenty-four hours dead drunk, not having waited for Christmas. In another corner of the room a wretched old woman of eighty, who had once been a children's nurse, but was now left to die friendless, was moaning and groaning with rheumatism, scolding and grumbling at the boy so that he was afraid to go near her corner. He had got a drink of water in the outer room, but could not find a crust anywhere, and had been on the point of waking his mother a dozen times. He felt frightened at last in the darkness; it had long been dusk, but no light was kindled. Touching his mother's face, he was surprised that she did not move at all, and that she was as cold as the wall. "It is very cold here," he thought. He stood a little, unconsciously letting his hands rest on the dead woman's shoulders, then he breathed on his fingers to warm them, and then quietly fumbling for his cap on the bed, he went out of the cellar. He would have gone earlier, but was afraid of the big dog which had been howling all day at the neighbour's door at the top of the stairs. But the dog was not there now, and he went out into the street.

Mercy on us, what a town! He had never seen anything like it before. In the town from which he had come, it was always such black darkness at night. There was one lamp for the whole street, the little, low-pitched, wooden houses were closed up with shutters, there was no one to be seen in the street after dusk, all the people shut themselves up in their houses, and there was nothing but the howling of packs of dogs, hundreds and thousands of them barking and howling all night. But there it was so warm and he was given food, while here—oh, dear, if he only had something to eat! And what a noise and rattle here, what light and what people, horses and carriages, and what a frost! The frozen steam hung in clouds over the horses, over their warmly breathing mouths; their hoofs clanged against the stones through the powdery snow, and everyone pushed so, and—oh, dear, how he longed for some morsel to eat, and how wretched he suddenly felt. A policeman walked by and turned away to avoid seeing the boy.

Here was another street—oh, what a wide one, here he would be run over for certain; how everyone was shouting, racing and driving along, and the light, the light! And what was this? A huge glass window, and through the window a tree reaching up to the ceiling; it was a fir tree, and on it were ever so many lights, gold papers and apples and little dolls and horses; and there were children clean and dressed in their best, running about the room, laughing and playing and eating and drinking something. And then a little girl began dancing with one of the boys; what a pretty little girl! And he could hear the music through the window. The boy looked and wondered and laughed, though his toes were aching with the cold and his fingers were red and stiff so that it hurt him to move them. And all at once the boy remembered how his toes and fingers hurt him, and began crying, and ran on; and again through another window-pane he saw another Christmas tree, and on a table cakes of all sorts—almond cakes, red cakes and yellow cakes, and three grand young ladies were sitting there, and they gave the cakes to anyone who went up to them, and the door kept opening; lots of gentlemen and ladies went in from the street. The boy crept up, suddenly opened the door and went in. Oh, how they shouted at him and waved him back! One lady went up to him hurriedly and slipped a kopeck into his hand, and with her own hands, opened the door into the street for him! How frightened he was. And the kopeck rolled away and clinked upon the steps; he could not bend his red fingers to hold it tight. The boy ran away and went on, where he did not know. He was ready to cry again, but he was afraid, and ran on and on and blew on his fingers. And he was miserable because he felt suddenly so lonely and terrified, and all at once, mercy on us! What was this again? People were standing in a crowd admiring. Behind a glass window there were three little dolls dressed in red and green dresses, and exactly, exactly as though they were alive. One was a little old man sitting and playing a big violin, the two others were standing close by and playing little violins and nodding in time, and looking at one another, and their lips moved. They were speaking, actually speaking, only one couldn't hear through the glass. And at first the boy thought they were alive, and when he grasped that they were dolls, he laughed. He had never seen such dolls before, and had no idea there were such dolls! And he wanted to cry, but he felt amused, amused by the dolls. All at once, he fancied that someone caught at his smock behind; a wicked big boy was standing beside him and suddenly hit him on the head, snatched off his cap, and tripped him up. The boy fell down on the ground and at once there was a shout. He was numb with fright, so he jumped up and ran away. He ran, and not knowing where he was going, ran in at the gate of someone's courtyard and sat down behind a stack of wood, "They won't find me here—besides it's dark!"

He sat huddled up and was breathless from fright, and all at once, quite suddenly, he felt so happy: his hands and feet suddenly left off aching and grew so warm, as warm as though he were on a stove; then he shivered all over, then he gave a start, why, he must have been asleep. How nice to have a sleep here! "I'll sit here a little and go and look at the dolls again," said the boy, and he smiled, thinking of them. "Just as though they were alive!..." And suddenly, he heard his mother singing over him. "Mammy, I am asleep. How nice it is to sleep here!"

"Come to my Christmas tree, little one," a soft voice suddenly whispered over his head.

He thought that this was still his mother, but no, it was not she. Who it was calling him, he could not see, but someone bent over and embraced him in the darkness; and he stretched out his hands to him, and—and all at once—oh, what a bright light! Oh, what a Christmas tree! And yet it was not a fir tree; he had never seen a tree like that! Where was he now? Everything was bright and shining, and all round him were dolls; but no, they were not dolls, they were little boys and girls, only so bright and shining. They all came flying round him, they all kissed him, took him, and carried him along with them, and he was flying himself, and he saw that his mother was looking at him and laughing joyfully. "Mammy, Mammy—oh, how nice it is here, Mammy!" And again he kissed the children and wanted to tell them at once of those dolls in the shop window. "Who are you, boys? Who are you, girls?" he asked, laughing and admiring them.

"This is Christ's Christmas tree," they answered. "Christ always has a Christmas tree on this day, for the little children who have no tree of their own…" And he found out that all these little boys and girls were children just like himself; that some had been frozen in the baskets in which they had as babies been laid on the doorsteps of well-to-do Petersburg people, others had been boarded out with Finnish women by the Foundling and had been suffocated, others had died at their starved mother's breasts (in the Samara famine), others had died in the third-class railway carriages from the foul air; and yet they were all here, they were all like angels about Christ, and He was in the midst of them and held out His hands to them and blessed them and their mothers… And the mothers of these children stood on one side weeping; each one knew her boy or girl, and the children flew up to them and kissed them and wiped away their tears with their little hands, and begged them not to weep because they were so happy.

And down below in the morning, the porter found the little dead body of the frozen child on the wood stack; they sought out his mother too… She had died before him. They met before the Lord God in heaven.

Why have I made up such a story, so out of keeping with an ordinary diary, and a writer's above all? And I promised two stories dealing with real events! But that is just it, I keep fancying that all this may have happened really—that is, what took place in the cellar and on the wood stack; but as for Christ's Christmas tree, I cannot tell you whether that could have happened or not.

Discussion Questions:
1. Why does Dostoevsky start the story with, "I am a novelist, and I suppose I have made up this story"?
2. The story ends the same way it began, with the narrator distancing himself from the events? Why is this?
3. Who was Fyodor Dostoevsky?

Writing Prompt:
　　When an author writes a story, their goal is to entertain while also sharing an idea. When we read, we want to be like a detective and find this idea. For fictional stories, this idea is frequently called the theme. Author's also include messages, morals, and lessons. Fyodor Dostoevsky is considered one of the greatest novelists of all time. Born in Russia in the 1800s, in his twenties he was thrown in prison for his political views and witnessed firsthand life's occasional brutality. His work reflects his

experience, and his writing regularly challenges us to think and question our beliefs. In "The Heavenly Christmas Tree," what is Dostoevsky wanting us to consider?

_____

_____

_____

_____

_____

_____

_____

_____

_____

_____

_____

_____

_____

_____

Chief Joseph "Nez Perces" 1880

Chief Joseph, 1883

Chief Joseph, Selected Speeches, 1874-1879

The following famous speeches were given by Chief Joseph of the Nez Perce between 1874-1879. In 1877, the Nez Pearce fled 1,700 miles to the Canadian border in an effort to escape being placed on permanent reservations. The tribe was captured forty miles from the border.

I.

The first white men of your people who came to our country were named Lewis and Clark. They brought many things which our people had never seen. They talked straight and our people gave them a great feast as proof that their hearts were friendly. They made presents to our chiefs, and our people made presents to them. We had a great many horses of which we gave them what they needed, and they gave us guns and tobacco in return. All the Nez Perce made friends with Lewis and Clark and agreed to let them pass through their country and never to make war on white men. This promise the Nez Perce have never broken.

II.

For a short time we lived quietly. But this could not last. White men had found gold in the mountains around the land of the Winding Water. They stole a great many horses from us and we could not get them back because we were Indians. The white men told lies for each other. They drove off a great many of our cattle. Some white men branded our young cattle so they could claim them. We had no friends who would plead our cause before the law councils. It seemed to me that some of the white men in Wallowa were doing these things on purpose to get up a war. They knew we were not stong enough to fight them. I labored hard to avoid trouble and bloodshed. We gave up some of our country to the white men, thinking that then we could have peace. We were mistaken. The white men would not let us alone. We could have avenged our wrongs many times, but we did not. Whenever the Government has asked for help against other Indians we have never refused. When the white men were few and we were strong, we could have killed them off, but the Nez Perce wishes to live at peace.

On account of the treaty made by the other bands of the Nez Perce, the white man claimed my lands. We were troubled with white men crowding over the line. Some of them were good men, and we lived on peaceful terms with them, but they were not all good. Nearly every year the agent came over from Lapwai and ordered us to the reservation. We always replied that we were satisfied to live in Wallowa. We were careful to refuse the presents or annuities which he offered.

Through all the years since the white man came to Wallowa, we have been threatened and taunted by them and the treaty Nez Perce. They have given us no rest. We have had a few good friends among the white men, and they have always advised my people to bear these taunts without fighting. Our young men are quick-tempered and I have had great trouble in keeping them from doing rash things. I have carried a heavy load on my back ever since I was a boy. I learned then that we were but few, while the white men were many, and that we could not hold our own with them. We were like deer. They were like grizzly bears. We had a small country. Their country was large. We were contented to let things remain as the Great Spirit Chief made them. They were not; and would change the mountains and rivers if they did not suit them.

III.
(During his surrender to U.S. cavalry in the Bear Paw Mountains, 1877)

Tell General Howard that I know his heart. What he told me before I have in my heart. I am tired of fighting. Our chiefs are killed. Looking Glass is dead, Tu-hul-hil-sote is dead. The old men are all dead. It is the young men who now say yes or no. He who led the young men [Joseph's brother Alikut] is dead. It is cold and we have no blankets. The little children are freezing to death. My people—some of them have run away to the hills and have no blankets and no food. No one knows where they are—perhaps freezing to death. I want to have time to look for my children and see how many of them I can find. Maybe I shall find them among the dead. Hear me, my chiefs, my heart is sick and sad. From where the sun now stands, I will fight no more against the white man.

IV.
(While visiting Washington, D.C., 1879]

At last I was granted permission to come to Washington and bring my friend Yellow Bull and our interpreter with me. I am glad I came. I have shaken hands with a good many friends, but there are some things I want to know which no one seems able to explain. I cannot understand how the Government sends a man out to fight us, as it did General Miles, and then breaks his word. Such a government has something wrong about it. I cannot understand why so many chiefs are allowed to talk so many different ways and promise so many different things. I have seen the Great Father Chief [President Hayes]; the Next Great Chief [Secretary of the Interior]; the Commissioner Chief; the Law Chief; and many other law chiefs [Congressmen] and they all say they are my friends, and that I shall have justice, but while all their mouths talk right, I do not understand why nothing is done for my people. I have heard talk and talk, but nothing is done. Good words do not last long unless they amount to something. Words do not pay for my dead people. They do not pay for my country now overrun by white men. They do not protect my father's grave. They do not pay for my horses and cattle. Good words do not give me back my children. Good words will not make good the promise of your war chief, General Miles. Good words will not give my people a home where they can live in peace and take care of themselves. I am tired of talk that comes to nothing. It makes my heart sick when I remember all the good words and all the broken promises. There has been too much talking by men who had no right to talk. Too many misinterpretations have been made; too many misunderstandings have come up between the white men and the Indians.

If the white man wants to live in peace with the Indian, he can live in peace. There need be no trouble. Treat all men alike. Give them the same laws. Give them all an even chance to live and grow. All men were made by the same Great Spirit Chief. They are all brothers. The earth is the mother of all people, and all people should have equal rights upon it. You might as well expect all rivers to run backward as that any man who was born a free man should be contented, penned up, and denied liberty to go where he pleases. If you tie a horse to a stake, do you expect he will grow fat? If you pen an Indian up on a small spot of earth and compel him to stay there, he will not be contented, nor will he grow and prosper. I have asked some of the Great White Chiefs where they get their authority to say to the Indian that he shall stay in one place, while he sees white men going where they please. They cannot tell me.

I only ask of the Government to be treated as all other men are treated. If I cannot go to my own home, let me have a home in a country where my people will not die so fast. I would like to go to Bitter Root Valley. There my people would be happy; where they are now, they are dying. Three have died since I left my camp to come to Washington.

When I think of our condition, my heart is heavy. I see men of my own race treated as outlaws and driven from country to country, or shot down like animals.

I know that my race must change. We cannot hold our own with the white men as we are. We only ask an even chance to live as other men live. We ask to be recognized as men. We ask that the same law shall work alike on all men. If an Indian breaks the law, punish him by the law. If a white man breaks the law, punish him also.

Let me be a free man, free to travel, free to stop, free to work, free to trade where I choose, free to choose my own teachers, free to follow the religion of my fathers, free to talk, think and act for myself—and I will obey every law or submit to the penalty.

Whenever the white man treats the Indian as they treat each other, then we shall have no more wars. We shall be all alike—brothers of one father and mother, with one sky above us and one country around us and one government for all. Then the Great Spirit Chief who rules above will smile upon this land and send rain to wash out the blood spots made by brothers' hands upon the face of the earth. For this time, the Indian race is waiting and praying. I hope no more groans of wounded men and women will ever go to the ear of the Great Spirit Chief above, and that all people may be one people.

Hin-mah-too-yah-lat-kekht has spoken for his people.

Discussion Questions:
1. Why are Chief Joseph's words still relevant nearly 150 years after they were spoken?
2. Are Chief Joseph's observations and accusations about the treatment of his people founded or unfounded? Why or why not?
3. Who was Chief Joseph?

Writing Prompt:
A speech always has a message. When we read, we want to be like a detective and find the message. In Chief Joseph's speeches, what is the message?

_____

_____

_____

_____

_____

_____

_____

_____

_____

_____

The Charge of the Light Brigade

By Alfred, Lord Tennyson

Half a league, half a league,
Half a league onward,
All in the valley of Death
Rode the six hundred.
'Forward, the Light Brigade!
Charge for the guns!' he said:
Into the valley of Death
Rode the six hundred.

'Forward, the Light Brigade!'
Was there a man dismay'd ?
Not tho' the soldier knew
Some one had blunder'd:
Their's not to make reply,
Their's not to reason why,

Their's but to do and die:
Into the valley of Death
Rode the six hundred.

Cannon to right of them,
Cannon to left of them,
Cannon in front of them
Volley'd and thunder'd;
Storm'd at with shot and shell,
Boldly they rode and well,
Into the jaws of Death,
Into the mouth of Hell
Rode the six hundred.

Flash'd all their sabres bare,
Flash'd as they turn'd in air
Sabring the gunners there,
Charging an army, while
All the world wonder'd:
Plunged in the battery-smoke
Right thro' the line they broke;
Cossack and Russian
Reel'd from the sabre-stroke
Shatter'd and sunder'd.
Then they rode back, but not
Not the six hundred.

Cannon to right of them,
Cannon to left of them,
Cannon behind them
Volley'd and thunder'd;
Storm'd at with shot and shell,
While horse and hero fell,
They that had fought so well
Came thro' the jaws of Death,
Back from the mouth of Hell,
All that was left of them,
Left of six hundred.
When can their glory fade?

O the wild charge they made!
All the world wonder'd.
Honour the charge they made!
Honour the Light Brigade,
Noble six hundred!

Discussion Questions:
1. How do you feel after reading this poem?
2. Where and why did this battle take place?
3. Who was Alfred, Lord Tennyson?

Writing Prompt:
Poetry can be described as "word art." Poets want to inspire, entertain, and share a message. Poets use specific words and word placement to accomplish this goal. For over 150 years, this poem has been appreciated for the imagery that brings the battle to life. Discuss the imagery and how it helps Tennyson share his message?

_____

_____

_____

_____

_____

_____

_____

_____

_____

Argument/Persuasive Writing: Mandatory Music Education

Not every student needs to play in an organized band, but is it reasonable for every teen to have at least some music education in the form of a mandatory music class?

Studies show that childhood brain development in the language areas of the brain increases when students are involved with music from a younger age. In addition, music gives students a better understanding of the world they live in. When students learn about and play music, they're much more susceptible to studying and learning about the cultures that foster the music they're studying and the instruments they're playing.

In addition, research demonstrates that studying music leads to better grades since studying music inherently leads students to think creatively and solve problems in order to play music. These skills then spill over into other subject areas.

However, mandatory music education will significantly raise the overall cost of education, and since core subjects like language skills and math are a priority, the budget for music is often limited. Indeed, in order for every student to have music education, the education budget would need to rise considerably to cover the need for purchasing instruments, hiring teachers, and maintaining facilities and instruments.

Time is another factor in music education. Where and how will schools and students find the time to add music education to a student's schedule?

With the obstacles opposing music education, it's easy to understand why it's not a mandatory subject. However, would it be wise to find the time and money to make music education a necessity?

Writing Prompt:

Is mandatory music education a reasonable idea? For evidence, state your experience, conduct research, conduct an interview, or include a survey.

_____

_____

_____

_____

_____

_____

_____

_____

_____

_____

_____

The Tale of the Little Bad Boy

By Mark Twain

Once there was a bad little boy whose name was Jim—though, if you will notice, you will find that bad little boys are nearly always called James in your Sunday school books. It was strange, but still it was true that this one was called Jim.

He didn't have any sick mother either—a sick mother who was pious and had the consumption, and would be glad to lie down in the grave and be at rest but for the strong love she bore her boy, and the anxiety she felt that the world might be harsh and cold towards him when she was gone. Most bad boys in the Sunday books are named James, and have sick mothers, who teach them to say, "Now, I lay me down," etc. and sing them to sleep with sweet, plaintive voices, and then kiss them goodnight, and kneel down by the bedside and weep. But it was different with this fellow. He was named Jim, and there wasn't anything the matter with his mother—no consumption, nor anything of that kind. She was rather stout than otherwise, and she was not pious; moreover, she was not anxious on Jim's account. She said if he were to break his neck it wouldn't be much loss. She always spanked Jim to sleep, and she never kissed him goodnight; on the contrary, she boxed his ears when she was ready to leave him.

Once this little bad boy stole the key of the pantry, and slipped in there and helped himself to some jam, and filled up the vessel with tar, so that his mother would never know the difference; but all at once a terrible feeling didn't come over him, and something didn't seem to whisper to him, "Is it right to disobey my mother? Isn't it sinful to do this? Where do bad little boys go who gobble up their good kind mother's jam?" and then he didn't kneel down all alone and promise never to be wicked any more, and rise up with a light, happy heart, and go and tell his mother all about it, and beg her forgiveness, and be blessed by her with tears of pride and thankfulness in her eyes. No, that is the way with all other bad boys in the books; but it happened otherwise with this Jim, strangely enough. He ate that jam, and said it was bully, in his sinful, vulgar way; and he put in the tar, and said that was bully also, and laughed, and observed "that the old woman would get up and snort" when she found it out; and when she did find it out, he denied knowing anything about it, and she whipped him severely, and he did the crying himself. Everything about this boy was curious—everything turned out differently with him from the way it does to the bad James in the books.

Once he climbed up in Farmer Acorn's apple tree to steal apples, and the limb didn't break, and he didn't fall and break his arm, and get torn by the farmer's great dog, and then languish on a sick bed for weeks, and repent and become good. Oh, no! He stole as many apples as he wanted and came down all right; and he was all ready for the dog too, and knocked him endways with a brick when he came to tear him. It was very strange—nothing like it ever happened in those mild little books with marbled backs, and with pictures in them of men with swallow-tailed coats and bell-crowned hats, and pantaloons that are short in the legs, and women with the waists of their dresses under their arms, and no hoops on. Nothing like it in any of the Sunday school books.

Once he stole the teacher's penknife, and, when he was afraid it would be found out and he would get whipped, he slipped it into George Wilson's cap—poor Widow Wilson's son, the moral boy, the good little boy of the village, who always obeyed his mother, and never told an untruth, and was fond of his lessons, and infatuated with Sunday school. And when the knife dropped from the cap, and poor George hung his head and blushed, as if in conscious guilt, and the grieved teacher charged the theft upon him, and was just in the very act of bringing the switch down upon his trembling shoulders, a white-haired improbable justice of the peace did not suddenly appear in their midst, and strike an attitude and say, "Spare this noble boy—there stands the cowering culprit! I was passing the school door at recess, and unseen myself, I saw the theft committed!" And then Jim didn't get whaled, and the venerable justice didn't read the tearful school a homily and take George by the hand and say such a boy deserved to be exalted, and then tell him to come and make his home with him, and sweep out the office, and make fires, and run errands, and chop wood, and study law, and help his wife to do household labors, and have all the balance of the time to play, and get forty cents a month, and be happy. No—it would have happened that way in the books, but it didn't happen that way to Jim. No meddling old clam of a justice dropped in to make trouble, and so the model boy George got thrashed, and Jim was glad of it because, you know, Jim hated moral boys. Jim said he was "down on them milk sops." Such was the coarse language of this bad, neglected boy.

But the strangest thing that ever happened to Jim was the time he went boating on Sunday, and didn't get drowned, and that other time that he got caught out in the storm when he was fishing on Sunday, and didn't get struck by lighting. Why, you might look, and look, all through the Sunday school books from now till next Christmas, and you would never come across anything like this. Oh no! You would find that all the bad boys who go boating on Sunday invariably get drowned; and all the bad boys who get caught out in storms when they are fishing on Sunday infallibly get struck by lightning. Boats with bad boys in them always upset on Sunday, and it always storms when bad boys go fishing on the Sabbath. How this Jim ever escaped is a mystery to me.

This Jim bore a charmed life—that must have been the way of it. Nothing could hurt him. He even gave the elephant in the menagerie a plug of tobacco, and the elephant didn't knock the top of his head off with his trunk. He browsed around the cupboard after essence of peppermint and didn't make a mistake and drink aqua fortis. He stole his father's gun and went hunting on the Sabbath, and didn't shoot three or four of his fingers off. He struck his little sister on the temple with his fist when he was angry, and she didn't linger in pain through long summer days, and die with sweet words of forgiveness upon her lips that redoubled the anguish of his breaking heart. No, she got over it. He ran off and went to sea at last, and didn't come back and find himself sad and alone in the world, his loved one's sleeping in the quiet churchyard, and the vine-embowered home of his boyhood tumbled down and gone to decay. Ah, no! He came home as drunk as a piper, and got into the station house the first thing.

And he grew up and married, and raised a large family, and brained them all with an axe one night, and got wealthy by all manner of cheating and rascality; and now he is the infernalist wickedest scoundrel in his native village, and is universally respected, and belongs to the Legislature.

So you see, there never was a bad James in the Sunday school books that had such a streak of luck as this sinful Jim with the charmed life.

Discussion Questions:
1. What is Twain's explanation for Jim becoming a "little bad boy" and how does Jim keep avoiding trouble?
2. What is ironic about the ending of the story?
3. Who was Mark Twain?

Writing Prompt:
   When an author writes a story, their goal is to entertain while also sharing an idea. When we read, we want to be like a detective and find this idea. For fictional stories, this idea is frequently called the theme. Author's also include messages, morals, and lessons. Twain is famous for using humor, wit, and irony to share his messages. What is Twain's message in this story?

_____

_____

_____

_____

_____

_____

Stand Tall to Succeed

Coming into this world is not easy, especially for giraffes.

Baby giraffes fall eight feet from their mother's womb to the ground, and then, after hopefully landing on their backs, they roll over onto their legs and take their first view of the world. Then, their welcome into the world comes directly from their mother, but it's not a kiss or warm embrace. The mother giraffe backs up and makes sure her baby is all right, and then she swiftly lifts her leg and swings it down at her baby.

The kick sends her baby somersaulting like a sack of flour across the ground. If her baby does not immediately stand on its hooves, the mother giraffe does the same thing again. She will keep kicking her baby until her baby stands on its hooves.

When the baby giraffe finally stands erect, only then will the mother show her baby tenderness. But then the mother again does something unexpected. She kicks her baby one last time and sends it somersaulting across the bare earth.

So why the perceived maltreatment? In life, struggles and obstacles are important.

The first few kicks show the baby that it needs to stand on its hooves, and the last kick reminds the baby that it needs to get there fast and stay on its hooves in order to survive. The saying, "Life is like a jungle," is no truer than on the savannah. Baby giraffes face constant threats, and they have to be able to get to their hooves and move fast. Like a buffalo calf that stays with the herd to keep safe from wolves, baby giraffes remain safe when they have the protection of the herd. Hyenas and lions are always on the lookout for an easy meal, and an unprotected baby giraffe fits the bill.

So, from a distance, the mother giraffe's actions seem cruel, but up close they have a direct and meaningful purpose. Her baby's life hangs in the balance.

Of course, this lesson is transferable to people. When we're born, we're not kicked by our mothers or chased by predators, but we must learn to overcome obstacles to enjoy success. Indeed, like the baby giraffe, standing up and staying on our feet is a necessity for achieving our goals.

Discussion Questions:
1. Why does the mother kick her baby?
2. Is the mother giraffe cruel to her baby?
3. How are a human's challenges similar to that of a giraffe's?

Writing Prompt:
Articles always have a main idea. When we read, we want to be like a detective and find the author's main idea. What is the main idea of this article?

_____

_____

_____

_____

_____

_____

He Wishes for the Cloths of Heaven

By William Butler Yeats

Had I the heavens' embroidered cloths,
Enwrought with golden and silver light,
The blue and the dim and the dark cloths
Of night and light and the half-light,
I would spread the cloths under your feet:
But I, being poor, have only my dreams;
I have spread my dreams under your feet;
Tread softly because you tread on my dreams.

Discussion Questions:
1. How do you feel after reading this poem?
2. What does Yeats mean when he says, "Tread softly because you tread on my dreams?"

3. Who was William Butler Yeats?

Writing Prompt:

      Poetry can be described as "word art." Poets want to inspire, entertain, and share a message. Poets use specific words and word placement to accomplish this goal. Yeats wrote this poem for the woman he loved. He asked her to marry him several times, but she never did. Yeats creates several metaphors in this poem. Choose one and discuss how this metaphor helps Yeats convey his message?

_____

_____

_____

_____

_____

_____

_____

_____

_____

_____

_____

Argument/Persuasive Writing: Social Media

This topic continues to foster heated debates. All around the world, we see instances of social media being used for positive and negative purposes. In the end, though, when considering social media, does it have a beneficial or harmful impact on teens?

Teens have been known to become addicted to social media apps and video games, but many have learned teamwork and other collaborative skills through social media.

We also see social media used for cyberbullying and intimidation, yet it's also used to unite peoples and countries.

Regarding our health, it's been well-documented that social media overuse and being influenced by it can lead to problems like eating and sleeping disorders.

In contrast, many apps can help people get healthier by assisting with exercise, weight loss, and concentration skills.

What do you think? In the grand scheme of things, do the advantages of social media outweigh its disadvantages?

Writing Prompt:
Is social media beneficial or harmful to teens? For evidence, state your experience, conduct research, conduct an interview, or include a survey.

The Owl and the Grasshopper

From *Aesop's Fables*

The Owl always takes her sleep during the day. Then, after sundown, when the rosy light fades from the sky and the shadows rise slowly through the wood, out she comes ruffling and blinking from the old hollow tree. Now her weird "hoo-hoo-hoo-oo-oo" echoes through the quiet wood, and she begins her hunt for the bugs and beetles, frogs and mice, she likes so well to eat.

Now, there was a certain old owl who had become very cross and hard to please as she grew older, especially if anything disturbed her daily slumbers. One warm summer afternoon as she dozed away in her den in the old oak tree, a grasshopper nearby began a joyous, but very raspy song. Out popped the old owl's head from the opening in the tree that served her both for door and for window.

"Get away from here, sir," she said to the grasshopper. "Have you no manners? You should at least respect my age and leave me to sleep in quiet!"

But the grasshopper answered saucily that he had as much right to his place in the sun as the owl had to her place in the old oak. Then he struck up a louder and still more rasping tune.

The wise old owl knew quite well that it would do no good to argue with the grasshopper, nor with anybody else for that matter. Besides, her eyes were not sharp enough by day to permit her to punish the grasshopper as he deserved. So she laid aside all hard words and spoke very kindly to him.

She said, "Well, sir, if I must stay awake, I'm going to settle right down to enjoy your singing. Now that I think of it, I have a wonderful wine here, sent to me from Olympus, of which I am told Apollo drinks before he sings to the high gods. Please come up and taste this delicious drink with me, and I know it will make you sing like Apollo himself."

The foolish grasshopper was taken in by the owl's words. Up he jumped to the owl's den, but as soon as he was near enough so the old owl could see him clearly, she pounced upon him and ate him up.

Discussion Questions:
1. Why does the owl become angry at the grasshopper?
2. Does the grasshopper deserve the fate he receives?
3. Who was Aesop? Why are his fables still read by children, teens, and adults three thousand years after they were written?

Writing Prompt:
When an author writes a story, their goal is to entertain while also sharing an idea. When we read, we want to be like a detective and find this idea. For fictional stories, this idea is frequently called the theme. Author's also include messages, morals, and lessons. What is the moral Aesop teaches in "The Owl and the Grasshopper"?

_____

_____

_____

_____

_____

_____

75

The World's Most Beautiful Tree

Like a magical tree from a fantasy or fable, the *Eucalyptus deglupta* will take your breath away with its otherworldly beauty. Nicknamed the "Rainbow" tree, it's recognized by many as "The World's Most Beautiful Tree." Yet like so many characters in fables, this remarkable tree has an unusual annual transformation from dull beast to stunning beauty.

The Rainbow tree is native to Southeast Asia, including the Philippines, New Guinea, and Indonesia. It's not too far of a stretch to say many people have fallen in love with this tree after seeing it for the first time. People revere these trees with the same admiration one might have for a painting by Michelangelo or Vincent Van Gogh, which seems somewhat understandable since the intense natural color is almost unreal.

In fact, many people who only see photos of the tree are skeptical. They rightfully think the blue, green, purple, orange, and red colors have been enhanced or doctored, but the colors are indeed real. And as strange as it may sound, to many the colors are not even the most surprising thing about this tree. Eucalyptus' are well known for their aromatic and astringent scent, but it's said that the *E. deglupta* is the most aromatic tree on earth. Its leaves, when crushed in the hand, have been known to leave the inhaler light-headed and euphoric from the pungent scent.

Southeast Asia is located in the Pacific Ocean between China and Australia. Indonesia, the Philippines, and New Guinea are the major island-countries in this section of the Pacific. The climate is humid and warm for much of the year. This temperate climate creates ideal conditions for the *E. deglupta* to thrive. The *E. deglupta* needs full sun, warm weather, and moist soil conditions.

So how do the unique colors appear? For a large part of the year, the bark is a dull shade of brown, yet at the start of summer, the tree begins its transformation. Similar to a snake shedding its skin, the tree starts shedding its outer bark once the warmer weather arrives. When the bark begins to shed, the lighter neon green flesh of the tree is exposed. Over the next few weeks, as the inner part of the tree comes in contact with oxygen, the green flesh turns the many

shades of blue, purple, orange, red and every other color of the rainbow that gives the tree its name. The tree will even change colors as the growing season continues, making for a continual and almost daily display of different shades of beauty.

However, once the growing season ends, again like a fable, the beauty fades and the tree takes on the dull brown beastly hue that it wears throughout the rest of the year. Fortunately, the transformation begins anew the following summer.

This surprising annual metamorphosis inspires and grabs our attention, but it appears the beauty is reserved for only those in Southeast Asia. Cultivators have taken seedlings and saplings and planted them elsewhere in cooler climates, and even imported native soils to plant the trees, but these orphans lack the beauty of those that grow in their native habitat. Indeed, when gardeners have tried to cultivate the tree in places like North America, the colors are mild and bland.

Regarding size, when given a fair amount of space, they will grow to their optimum trunk diameter of six feet and height of 250 feet. The trees are also one of the fastest growing trees in the world. Typically, they grow three feet each year, but some specimens have been known to grow almost twenty feet in a year. The balmy growing conditions of the islands helps facilitate this speedy growth.

Like other eucalyptus trees, the *E. deglupta's* six-inch tapered leaves are about four inches wide. These leaves, especially when crushed, emit the astringent and pungent aroma associated with all eucalyptus trees. The tree also grows small white flower blossoms throughout the year.

Outside of their amazing visual appeal, these trees have several uses. They are regularly used in urban and rural areas for landscaping among homes, ranches, gardens, buildings, and recreational facilities. In addition, large plantations across Southeast Asia grow the trees to be a source of pulpwood, which is used to make paper and paper products.

Photo by Amelia

Moreover, the *E. deglupta* is used as a source of hardwood for lumber, furniture, cabinets, boats, railings, and natural decking material. The natural oils found in the wood help preserve it from the elements.

In some areas, the tree is even planted for health reasons. Each tree soaks up an inordinate amount of water each day, so they are planted in areas of swampy, standing water. This helps prevent mosquitoes from breeding, which limits the spread of mosquito-borne malaria.

All in all, the striking appearance of the *Eucalyptus deglupta* is a delight to behold. It's a rare and somewhat finicky specimen, yet like a fable, the magic and beauty will come as long as it has just the right conditions to bring it back to life.

Discussion Questions:
1. Where and what is the *Eucalyptus deglupta's* native habitat?
2. Why doesn't the *E. deglupta* thrive in northern climates?
3. Other than its beauty, what are some of the *E. deglupta's* other useful traits?

Writing Prompt:
Articles always have a main idea. When we read, we want to be like a detective and find the author's main idea. What is the main idea of this article?

The White Buffalo (excerpt)

It's nearly impossible to survive on the open plain without shelter. Similar to a sailor adrift on the ocean, the wind and sun steal the life from any unfortunate soul who wanders the prairie unprepared.

A novice can survive a week without shelter, but any longer and they will not only succumb to the elements, they will first lose their grip on reality since there are few landmarks to offer the newcomer an anchor to the world. From one horizon to its direct opposite, much of the great plains is flat. Without landmarks, the terrain becomes otherworldly. The expansiveness and harshness swallow the mind.

Facing such a situation, humans quickly realize the land is the master. Unfortunately, for the lost or foolish ones, there is no second chance at learning: the plains simply consume those who do not belong there.

However, having grown up on the plains, Eagle Feather and Wild Horse knew to honor the prairie and not try to outlast it, so like those that came before them, each headed immediately to mountains for shelter. Eagle Feather sought the mountains that lay to the north, while Wild Horse journeyed to the mountains in the south.

Eagle Feather had a shorter journey, as the mountains were about fifteen miles away, but he had to maneuver over hills and through several slot canyons. Wild Horse, on the other hand, had a straight run across the prairie of twenty miles.

Eagle Feather crossed the low-lying hills, scrambled past thickets of scrub brush, and kept climbing until he reached the higher elevations where plentiful white-barked aspens and tall pines grew. The forest was thick with pine scent. He came upon a stand of Lodgepole pines adjacent to a small meandering creek, stopped, and inhaled deeply.

"This is the place," he said aloud.

His buckskin was moist with sweat, so he pulled the shirt over his head and hung it over a nearby tree limb. The cool breeze revived him. He reached back and removed the leather thongs holding his two braids. He ran strong hands through his hair, stopped to scrub his scalp, and then let his hair fall free. The breeze picked up his long, dark mane like a sail. Eagle Feather leaned his head back and gazed at the tips of the pines slowly swaying in the gentle breeze. He smiled. This was definitely the spot.

He looked around. The stream dissected a meadow a stone's throw in width, with the pines creating a circular border around the meadow. Ankle-high verdant green alpine grass covered the ground.

Across the creek and directly ahead of him, a large granite boulder about the size of a small cabin lay half-buried in the side of a hill. He immediately decided the rock itself would make for one side of an effective shelter, while gathered pine branches would make the other side of the lean-to.

He allowed himself a few minutes of rest before getting to work.

Then he gathered a few rocks from the stream and made a large fire ring several feet from the water. Next, he set to gathering pine branches that were lying on the ground. He sought branches that were about eight feet in length.

He soon began clearing away the pine needles and small rocks from the space that would be the floor of the shelter. He leaned each pole carefully at an angle against the boulder and then churned the ground end into the earth to secure the pole. Wispy aspen branches, leaves, and pine needles were stuffed between the poles to help shore-up the roof. At one end of the shelter, he placed a few gray rocks he had removed from the floor of the shelter in a circle to create a small fire ring for warmth while he slept. Within a matter of hours, Eagle Feather had an effective shelter to sit comfortably, sleep, and even enjoy a small fire.

Sleep came quickly that night.

The next morning, he set a rabbit snare. Finding a rabbit path was easy since the diminutive creatures frequented the stream. He then gathered three sticks about eighteen inches in length and one inch in diameter. He snapped off the ends so two of the sticks had y-shaped tips. The opposing ends of these two sticks were driven straight into the ground on either side of the path while the third stick became a horizontal pole sitting in the nooks created by the y-joints. After that, he cut a length of leather from his loincloth and fashioned a long string. He tied one end of the string to the horizontal pole directly over the rabbit path, let the string hang free, and then looped it back to itself just under the pole and tied the string to itself with a slip knot. The string was now a noose. When a rabbit hopped through the loop, its body weight would pull the noose tight, quickly killing the rabbit.

Throughout the morning, Eagle Feather waited patiently. By midday, he had had no success, so a lunch of beetle larvae sufficed to stave off the hunger pangs. Dinner was the same.

But the next morning, a hapless squirrel leaped to the ground from a nearby tree, took two quick steps, and then bounded right into the waiting leash. Eagle Feather had his first proper meal. Roasted on the fire, the squirrel was one of the finest meals Eagle Feather had ever eaten. Hunger, along with pride at making his first kill while on his journey, made the squirrel rival a great buffalo feast.

Over the next week, the snare nabbed three rabbits and one more squirrel. In addition, Eagle Feather caught two small trout in the stream. He had fashioned a small fish pen, but the trap was always bare when he checked. Instead, patience and quick hands had secured the fish. However, the trout were few and far between. Bugs made up the rest of his diet. Eagle Feather had dropped ten pounds by the end of the week. He felt the need to make a bigger kill. He decided to go deer hunting.

A large part of the ritual Eagle Feather was now doing was the vision quest. Eagle Feather's plan was to sit in the lean-to and meditate, awaiting Great Spirit to speak to or reveal himself directly to him. But Eagle Feather felt that in order to accomplish the quest and have the energy to return home safely, he needed a more effective food source. A deer would be perfect. He could bulk back up before going on the quest, make a rack to dry the rest of the meat, and when he finished the quest, he would have a ready food supply.

The night before the hunt, clouds gathered and poured icy rain for two hours. However, Eagle Feather was secure in his lean-to. The roof held fairly well even though continual drops and later streams of water worked their way through the thatch roof. Eagle Feather had covered himself with a thick layer of insulating pine needles and oak leaves, so the downpour was tolerable.

In the morning, Eagle Feather crawled out of the hut and stretched. The fresh, moist scent of pine filled his lungs.

"Great Spirit guides me," he said aloud as he strode out of the meadow.

He had been hiking for only a few minutes when he spied a deer run. These trails were created by deer in search of food and water. The runs were like freeways, paths to water holes, creeks, and feeding pastures. The trail wound its way through a dense cedar grove. Eagle Feather had to get on his hands and knees to crawl at times. By the time the trail led out of the grove, Eagle Feather's hands were covered with the waxy film that coats each needle-like leaf.

After the grove, the trail veered to the right, and a wide vista opened up. From where Eagle Feather stood, the mountain ran down at a steep 45-degree angle in dark slopes of loose shale. Small islands of white and gray granite protruded from the shale and allowed diminutive pines and cedars to take precarious root.

Up from the trail, the mountain angle was less harsh, which allowed various pines and aspens to take root. The ground became soil as the trail ventured upward at a gentle slope. Once Eagle Feather hit soil, which allowed for positive footing, he climbed up and stayed about thirty feet up from the run. He then paralleled it so as not to alert the deer. In half a mile, the smaller pines and scrub brush gave way to dominant ponderosas. Standing about thirty to forty feet from each other, the trees had massive wingspans.

Eagle Feather stood at the base of one tree, stuck his nose in between the rows of deep crevassed red bark, and inhaled. The sweet aroma, like cookies baking, greeted his nostrils. "Thank you, Grandfather," he said.

He turned and peered out to the open spaces and plain below. From such a distance, the verdant plain looked like turf and ran to the east and south in unending greens. Peaks to the north resembled the mountain he stood on. Eagle Feather knew he was an ant in a universe of possibility.

Discussion Questions:
1. In the beginning of this excerpt, why are the plains compared to the sea? What is similar about the two?
2. How does Eagle Feather go about obtaining food?
3. What is the goal of his quest?

Writing Prompt:
        In this excerpt from *The White Buffalo*, Eagle Feather has left his village and began his "right of manhood." At the excerpt's beginning, we learn the plains can be as harsh as the open ocean. Why are the plains so dangerous to those who are unfamiliar with its pitfalls?

_____

_____

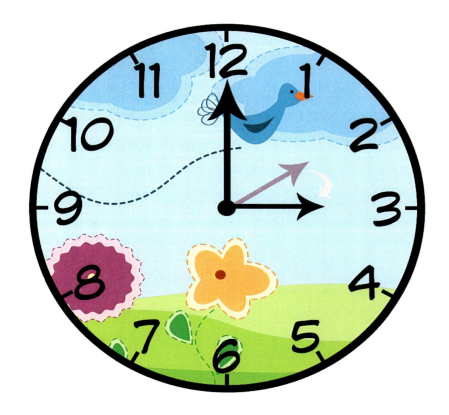

Argument/Persuasive Writing: Four-Day Work Week

A five-day work week has been a part of our culture for over one hundred years. This length of work week began in the late 1900's because of the industrial revolution. Before that, we were a farm-based culture, so every day, except Sunday, was a workday.

Today, with so many people doing many different types of work, some people believe we would be more productive if we had a four-day work week.

Proponents suggest that it would be better to work for ten-hours-per-day four-days-per-week rather than working the traditional model of eight-hours-per-day five-days-per-week. This includes students in school. They think that three days off would help students rest more so that they could be more productive during the ten-hour days.

Opponents believe that the current model is fine. They state that ten-hours-per-day of work is not constructive. They believe that this is too long of a workday for many adults, let alone students. Plus, they argue that a longer day takes away from after-school activities and family time.

What do you think?

Writing Prompt:

Is a four-day work week a good idea? For evidence, state your experience, conduct research, conduct an interview, or include a survey.

_____

_____

_____

_____

_____

_____

_____

_____

_____

_____

_____

_____

_____

APPENDIX

Essay Prompts

The primary objective of *The Baran Method* is to give students the tools and structure needed to become a successful academic writer.

Working on **C****E****A** paragraphs gives students time to practice mastering these tools and the associated structure.

Once paragraph writing is mastered, students are prepared to turn a **C****E****A** paragraph into the body paragraph(s) of an essay. This progression allows for confidence to grow as students begin to understand the fundamentals of successful essay writing.

If students are struggling with or new to essay writing, begin with a short three-paragraph essay. When students feel comfortable writing more, progress to a four-paragraph essay, and then progress to a five-paragraph essay and beyond.

By the completion of tenth grade, the goal is for students to have acquired a solid understanding of essay writing and structure so they can begin to make their essay paragraphs more complex as they progress through the grade levels.

Remember to use the easy-to-follow essay maps in *The Baran Method: Writing for Success* to guide students sentence-by-sentence as they write each sentence of their essay. Also, please refer to and use the example essays in this Teacher Edition and in the Online Resources as models for students to follow. Additional helpful resources including "How-To" videos, three and four-paragraph essay maps, lesson plans, and writing prompts can be found in the Online Resources at thebaranmethod.com/resources-access.

Finally, when writing essays, feel free to encourage the use of outside sources in addition to these workbook readings. Learning how to incorporate multiple sources while writing an essay is a necessary skill students need to master. However, begin slowly. As with all writing, allow time for students to gain confidence before accelerating the pace and intensity of instruction. Meeting students at their current skill level, and then gradually increasing the level of difficulty, is key to their writing success.

- "Crater of Fire" shares information about this unusual place. In a multi-paragraph essay, discuss *The Door to Hell*. For instance, how was it created, what danger does it present, and what are possible solutions? After you make each one of these questions the focus of a single body paragraph, so that you have a total of three body paragraphs, and then add an introduction and conclusion, you'll have written a five-paragraph essay. Feel free to include outside sources.

- "I'm Nobody! Who Are You?" is a classic. In a multi-paragraph essay, discuss the message and the figurative language Dickinson uses.

- In a multi-paragraph essay, discuss whether or not it's a good idea to ban junk from schools. For **evidence**, state your experience, conduct research, conduct an interview, or include a survey. You'll want to write two body paragraphs that focus solely on your position, and then, in the last body paragraph, write about the opposing viewpoint so that you show a balanced perspective. After you add an introduction and conclusion, you'll have written a five-paragraph essay.

- "The Monkey's Paw" is a spooky and entertaining classic. In a multi-paragraph essay, discuss the theme of this story. **An example of this essay is included in the Teacher Edition.**

- Steve Jobs is remembered for his visionary innovations. In a multi-paragraph essay, discuss his achievements. For instance, write about his work with Apple, Pixar, and the iPhone. After you make each one of these questions the focus of a single body paragraph, so that you have a total of three body paragraphs, and then add an introduction and conclusion, you'll have written a five-paragraph essay. Feel free to include outside sources. **An example of this essay is included in the Teacher Edition and the "Workbook Writing Examples" folder in the Online Resources.**

- In a multi-paragraph essay, discuss whether or not celebrities make effective role models. For **evidence**, state your experience, conduct research, conduct an interview, or include a survey. You'll want to write two body paragraphs that focus solely on your position, and then, in the last body paragraph, write about the opposing viewpoint so that you show a balanced perspective. After you add an introduction and conclusion, you'll have written a five-paragraph essay.

- One of the most brilliant thinkers and novelists of all time, Fyodor Dostoevsky, wrote "The Heavenly Christmas Tree." In a multi-paragraph essay, discuss the theme of this story.

- Chief Joseph's speeches are some of the most important speeches of all time. Who was Chief Joseph? Why are his words significant? Why does his message endure? After you make each one of these questions the focus of a single body paragraph, so that you have a total of three body paragraphs, and then add an introduction and conclusion, you'll have written a five-paragraph essay.

- "The Charge of the Light Brigade" was written by a literary icon, Alfred, Lord Tennyson. Tennyson uses figurative language throughout the piece. In a multi-paragraph essay, discuss Tennyson's use of imagery to convey his message.

- Mark Twain's "The Tale of the Little Bad Boy" is a humorous classic full of satirical wit. In a multi-paragraph essay, discuss Twain's message.

- In a multi-paragraph essay, discuss whether or not social media is beneficial for teenagers. For **evidence**, state your experience, conduct research, conduct an interview, or include a survey. You'll want to write two body paragraphs that focus solely on your position, and then, in the last body paragraph, write about the opposing viewpoint so that you show a balanced perspective. After you add an introduction and conclusion, you'll have written a five-paragraph essay. **An example of this essay is included in the Teacher Edition.**

- In a multi-paragraph essay, discuss *E. deglupta*. What causes its unique appearance, what are its uses, and why is it difficult to cultivate outside of its native environment? Feel free to include outside sources.

- In a multi-paragraph essay, discuss whether or not a four-day work week would be more productive. For **evidence**, state your experience, conduct research, conduct an interview, or include a survey. You'll want to write two body paragraphs that focus solely on your position, and then, in the last body paragraph, write about the opposing viewpoint so that you show a balanced perspective. After you add an introduction and conclusion, you'll have written a five-paragraph essay.

- Choose two poems from this workbook and compare and contrast the figurative language used in each.

- Choose two stories from this workbook and compare and contrast the themes.

- Several recurring themes occur throughout the readings in this workbook. Using one or two readings from the workbook, write a multi-paragraph essay that explores one of these themes.

- We continually deal with challenges in life. Using evidence from one, two, or three of these readings, write an essay that describes how the character/subject/author deals with challenges.

Helpful Websites

This is a list of helpful websites with student-friendly tools, articles, and activities. Also, remember to contact us if you have any questions. No question is insignificant—we love every question! You can email us at greg@thebaranmethod.com or call Ph. (760) 459-5597. Plus, we offer online writing courses and other helpful resources at thebaranmethod.com. We want your kids to succeed!

THEBARANMETHOD.COM

The home of *The Baran Method* for schools and careers that require writing (which is almost every career). You'll find our list of products, online courses, upcoming schedules for in-person and online events, tutorial videos, tips for better teaching, updates, and all kinds of useful information to help make learning how to write and teaching writing easier.

KAMIAPP.COM

FREE. Upload any PDF and then your child can annotate that document online with Kami's highlighters, text boxes, and colorful online tools.

MINDMEISTER.COM

FREE. A great brainstorming app. Your child can use the colorful bubble maps to generate and organize their ideas.

STORYLINEONLINE.NET

FREE. Actors and performers read well-known children's books. The site's creators add a small bit of fun animation to each story. A terrific resource to have in your bag to help your kids get interested in reading.

AMERICANLITERATURE.COM

FREE. An extensive collection of classic literature that's in the public domain. You'll find short stories, novels, poems, essays, and much more. Readings for all age-levels from young children to adults. A terrific resource for teachers looking to augment their curriculum with classic, traditional literature.

PROWRITINGAID.COM

FREE. This online editor offers lots of helpful features. You can upload a document right into it. It's easy to use, and when you're looking to work with grammar, it does a very effective job of showing errors without making you pay for editing.

DICTIONARY.COM/THESAURUS.COM

FREE. An excellent resource for definitions and synonyms. Click either tab for Dictionary.com or Thesaurus.com to alternate between the two as needed.

Writing Examples

The following examples are possible responses to the first four assignments in this workbook. Use each example to guide students. You can show students before they start writing, or use it as a guide while they're writing.

Remember, the goal when students begin writing is for them to learn the method—blue, green, and red—CEA. Students' initial responses will most likely be plain and simple. That's frustrating for some adults since they have an unmet expectation that their students should write like Shakespeare right away. But give it time. Instead, we want students to just practice getting their ideas on paper in a structured manner. Clarity of thought, increased vocabulary, and grammar comprehension will follow as writers continue to practice putting their ideas on paper.

"Hospital Window"

Three-Sentence CEA Paragraph

The theme of "Hospital Window" is that it is always best to help others. After the blind man passes away, the surviving patient asks the nurse why his friend would lie to him, and the nurse responds, "Maybe he just wanted to encourage you." This quote shows that the nurse understands the empathy the blind man showed to his friend, and that the blind man simply wanted to uplift and inspire his friend even while staring down his own death.

The theme of "Hospital Window" is that it is always best to help others. After the blind man passes away, the surviving patient asks the nurse why his friend would lie to him, and the nurse responds, "Maybe he just wanted to encourage you." This quote shows that the nurse understands the empathy the blind man showed to his friend, and that the blind man simply wanted to uplift and inspire his friend even while staring down his own death.

Five-Sentence CEA Paragraph

The theme of "Hospital Window" is that it is always best to help others. In the story, two severely ill men are in a hospital room, and one of the men describes the wonderful sights outside their hospital window to the other, even though the sights are figments of the man's imagination since he is blind. After the blind man passes away, the surviving patient asks the nurse why his friend would lie to him, and the nurse responds, "Maybe he just wanted to encourage you." This quote shows that the nurse understands the empathy the blind man showed to his friend, and that the blind man simply wanted to uplift and inspire his friend even while staring down his own death. Therefore, the theme teaches that sacrificing and helping others, even when we have very little to give, is one of the great gifts we can share with others.

The theme of "Hospital Window" is that it is always best to help others. In the story, two severely ill men are in a hospital room, and one of the men describes the wonderful sights outside their hospital window to the other, even though the sights are figments of the man's imagination since he is blind. After the blind man passes away, the surviving patient asks the nurse why his friend would lie to him, and the nurse responds, "Maybe he just wanted to encourage you." This quote shows that the nurse understands the empathy the blind man showed to his friend, and that the blind man simply wanted to uplift and inspire his friend even while staring down his own death. Therefore, the theme teaches that sacrificing and helping others, even when we have very little to give, is one of the great gifts we can share with others.

"Crater of Fire"

Three-Sentence CEA Paragraph

The main idea of "Crater of Fire" is that it would be wise for humankind to be cautious when dealing with nature since it is powerful and its laws supersede our needs. The article states, "Fifty years ago, while Turkmenistan was still part of the Soviet Union, Soviet geologists and engineers in search of crude oil trekked to a region of the Karakum Desert called Darvaza. The researchers had traveled to Darvaza as many geologists theorized there was a rich reserve of crude oil under the desert." This passage reveals that the geologists' quest was motivated by the search for oil, but in their haste, they caused the disaster now known as *The Door to Hell*.

The main idea of "Crater of Fire" is that it would be wise for humankind to be cautious when dealing with nature since it is powerful and its laws supersede our needs. The article states, "Fifty years ago, while Turkmenistan was still part of the Soviet Union, Soviet geologists and engineers in search of crude oil trekked to a region of the Karakum Desert called Darvaza. The researchers had traveled to Darvaza as many geologists theorized there was a rich reserve of crude oil under the desert." This passage reveals that the geologists' quest was motivated by the search for oil, but in their haste, they caused the disaster now known as *The Door to Hell.*

Five-Sentence CEA Paragraph

The main idea of "Crater of Fire" is that it would be wise for humankind to be cautious when dealing with nature since it is powerful and its laws supersede our needs. Along these lines, *The Door to Hell* was inadvertently created by scientists in search of oil. The article states, "Fifty years ago, while Turkmenistan was still part of the Soviet Union, Soviet geologists and engineers in search of crude oil trekked to a region of the Karakum Desert called Darvaza. The researchers had traveled to Darvaza as many geologists theorized there was a rich reserve of crude oil under the desert." This passage reveals that the geologists' quest was motivated by the search for oil, but in their haste, they caused the disaster now known as *The Door to Hell.* Consequently, we need what the earth provides to sustain us, but it would be beneficial in the future to be cautious how we proceed as we seek to utilize these resources.

The main idea of "Crater of Fire" is that it would be wise for humankind to be cautious when dealing with nature since it is powerful and its laws supersede our needs. Along these lines, *The Door to Hell* was inadvertently created by scientists in search of oil. The article states, "Fifty years ago, while Turkmenistan was still part of the Soviet Union, Soviet geologists and engineers in search of crude oil trekked to a region of the Karakum Desert called Darvaza. The researchers had traveled to Darvaza as many geologists theorized there was a rich reserve of crude oil under the desert." This passage reveals that the geologists' quest was motivated by the search for oil, but in their haste, they caused the disaster now known as *The Door to Hell.* Consequently, we need what the earth provides to sustain us, but it would be beneficial in the future to be cautious how we proceed as we seek to utilize these resources.

"I'm Nobody! Who are you?" By Emily Dickinson

*Please note the slant denoting the separation of lines in the poem. This punctuation format is associated with poetry analysis.

Three-Sentence CEA Paragraph

Dickinson compares society to frogs showing that striving to be popular is a waste of time. Dickinson writes, "How dreary – to be – Somebody! / How public – like a Frog – / To tell one's name – the livelong June – / To an admiring Bog!" Dickinson is saying that trying to be popular and fit in is foolish since people that place value on trying to be like others are like frogs croaking in an insignificant chorus.

Dickinson compares society to frogs showing that striving to be popular is a waste of time. Dickinson writes, "How dreary – to be – Somebody! / How public – like a Frog – / To tell one's name – the livelong June – / To an admiring Bog!" Dickinson is saying that trying to be popular and fit in is foolish since people that place value on trying to be like others are like frogs croaking in an insignificant chorus.

Five-Sentence CEA Paragraph

Dickinson compares society to frogs showing that striving to be popular is a waste of time. In the poem, Dickinson describes what it feels like to be an outcast, but she also says it is better to be an outcast than to change who we are to fit in. Dickinson writes, "How dreary – to be – Somebody! / How public – like a Frog – / To tell one's name – the livelong June – / To an admiring Bog!" Dickinson is saying that trying to be popular and fit in is foolish since people that place value on trying to be like others are like frogs croaking in an insignificant chorus. As a result, Dickinson's metaphor is powerful since it serves to remind us to live our lives according to our own values and not according to others.

Dickinson compares society to frogs showing that striving to be popular is a waste of time. In the poem, Dickinson describes what it feels like to be an outcast, but she also says it is better to be an outcast than to change who we are to fit in. Dickinson writes, "How dreary – to be – Somebody! / How public – like a Frog – / To tell one's name – the livelong June – / To an admiring Bog!" Dickinson is saying that trying to be popular and fit in is foolish since people that place value on trying to be like others are like frogs croaking in an insignificant chorus. As a result, Dickinson's metaphor is powerful since it serves to remind us to live our lives according to our own values and not according to others.

Junk Food Ban

*In the **Beyond the Five-Sentence CEA Paragraph** section below, there are two sentences in the **analysis** section. This is highly desirable, and it's what we want students to be able to do. Once students can confidently and competently write a CEA paragraph, we want them to expand their ideas and writing, which leads students down the path to developing their intellectual and creative abilities. When students ask if they can add more supporting details, evidence, and/or analysis, they have shown that they are headed toward a solid understanding and mastery of *The Baran Method* and they are ready for expanded writing. Adding more analysis is a solid first-step to take on this expanded writing journey.

Three-Sentence CEA Paragraph

It is not a good idea to ban junk food from schools. After interviewing several students, the overall consensus was that students have their own likes and dislikes regarding food and forcing them to eat a particular food will only force them to throw food away or not eat at all. Moreover, some students said they would just sneak food into school. Also, several students said that when the school has tried to implement healthy food days, the food is unappetizing, so if junk food is going to be banned, schools need to make sure the replacement food tastes good. This shows that while banning junk food and replacing it with healthier foods is a worthwhile idea, students are particular about what they eat and they strongly prefer to have a choice.

It is not a good idea to ban junk food from schools. After interviewing several students, the overall consensus was that students have their own likes and dislikes regarding food and forcing them to eat a particular food will only force them to throw food away or not eat at all. Moreover, some students said they would just sneak food into school. Also, several students said that when the school has tried to implement healthy food days, the food is unappetizing, so if junk food is going to be banned, schools need to make sure the replacement food tastes good. This shows that while banning junk food and replacing it with healthier foods is a worthwhile idea, students are particular about what they eat and they strongly prefer to have a choice.

Five-Sentence CEA Paragraph

It is not a good idea to ban junk food from schools. Everyone has the right to choose what they eat and drink, and if they choose junk food, that is their choice. After interviewing several students, the overall consensus was that students have their own likes and dislikes regarding food and forcing them to eat a particular food will only force them to throw food away or not eat at all. Moreover, some students said they would just sneak food into school. Also, several students said that when the school has tried to implement healthy food days, the food is unappetizing, so if junk food is going to be banned, schools need to make sure the replacement food tastes good. This shows that while banning junk food and replacing it with healthier foods is a worthwhile idea, students are particular about what they eat and they strongly prefer to have a choice. For these reasons, schools need to think about the consequences of banning or not banning junk food.

It is not a good idea to ban junk food from schools. Everyone has the right to choose what they eat and drink, and if they choose junk food, that is their choice. After interviewing several students, the overall consensus was that students have their own likes and dislikes regarding food and forcing them to eat a particular food will only force them to throw food away or not eat at all. Moreover, some students said they would just sneak food into school. Also, several students said that when the school has tried to implement healthy food days, the food is unappetizing, so if junk food is going to be banned, schools need to make sure the replacement food tastes good. This shows that while banning junk food and replacing it with healthier foods is a worthwhile idea, students are particular about what they eat and they strongly prefer to have a choice. For these reasons, schools need to think about the consequences of banning or not banning junk food.

Beyond the Five-Sentence CEA Paragraph

It is not a good idea to ban junk food from schools. Everyone has the right to choose what they eat and drink, and if they choose junk food, that is their choice. After interviewing several students, the overall consensus was that students have their own likes and dislikes regarding food and forcing them to eat a particular food will only force them to throw food away or not eat at all. Moreover, some students said they would just sneak food into school. Also, several students said that when the school has tried to implement healthy food days, the food is unappetizing, so if junk food is going to be banned, schools need to make sure the replacement food tastes good. This shows that while banning junk food and replacing it with healthier foods is a worthwhile idea, students are particular about what they eat and they strongly prefer to have a choice. In addition, students make a valuable point in that schools need to offer a wide variety of healthy and good tasting food if they are going to convert students over to being healthier eaters. For these reasons, schools need to think about the consequences of banning or not banning junk food.

It is not a good idea to ban junk food from schools. Everyone has the right to choose what they eat and drink, and if they choose junk food, that is their choice. After interviewing several students, the overall consensus was that students have their own likes and dislikes regarding food and forcing them to eat a particular food will only force them to throw food away or not eat at all. Moreover, some students said they would just sneak food into school. Also, several students said that when the school has tried to implement healthy food days, the food is unappetizing, so if junk food is going to be banned, schools need to make sure the replacement food tastes good. This shows that while banning junk food and replacing it with healthier foods is a worthwhile idea, students are particular about what they eat and they strongly prefer to have a choice. In addition, students make a valuable point in that schools need to offer a wide variety of healthy and good tasting food if they are going to convert students over to being healthier eaters. For these reasons, schools need to think about the consequences of banning or not banning junk food.